A
SPACE
SCIENCE
Journey

EXPLORE THE COSMOS
LIKE NEIL DeGRASSE TYSON

CAP Saucier

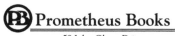 Prometheus Books

59 John Glenn Drive
Amherst, New York 14228

Published 2015 by Prometheus Books

Cover image © Shutterstock
Cover design by Nicole Somer-Lecht

Inquiries should be addressed to
Prometheus Books
59 John Glenn Drive
Amherst, New York 14228
VOICE: 716–691–0133
FAX: 716–691–0137
WWW.PROMETHEUSBOOKS.COM

19 18 17 16 15   5 4 3 2 1

Library of Congress Cataloging-in-Publication Data

Saucier, C. A. P., 1954-
   Explore the cosmos like Neil DeGrasse Tyson : a space science journey/by C.A.P. Saucier.
        pages cm
   Includes bibliographical references and index.
   ISBN 978-1-63388-014-6 (pbk.) — ISBN 978-1-63388-015-3 (ebook)
   1. Tyson, Neil deGrasse. 2. Astronomers—United States—Biography.
3. Astrophysicists—United States—Biography. 4. Astronomy—Popular works. I. Title.

QB36.T97S28 2015
520.92—dc23
[B]
                                                                     2014039219

Printed in the United States of America

I dedicate this book to my family.
We may have originated on different parts of this planet,
but we are all made of the same starstuff.

Be humble for you are made of Earth.
Be noble for you are made of stars.

—Serbian proverb

CONTENTS

Neil at age fourteen attending an astronomy camp in the Mojave Desert. *(Courtesy of Neil deGrasse Tyson)*

Chapter 1

A YOUNG SCIENTIST LOOKS AT THE SKY

"Hello, police? I'd like to report a burglar on the roof of the apartment building next to mine." Responding to the call, a police officer arrived at the high-rise apartments in the Bronx, New York, and made his way to the roof. When he reached the top, the officer may have wondered or laughed at the sight of the teenage boy he found looking through a telescope. But when that boy showed him the surface of the moon and then Saturn and its rings, the police officer left feeling that climbing up to the roof had been worth it, even if there was no criminal to catch. A person never forgets seeing Saturn for the first time.

That teenage boy with his telescope was Neil deGrasse Tyson, now a prominent astrophysicist. As a child, Neil's head was in the sky. He fell in love with the night sky when he was nine years old. By age eleven, he knew that he wanted to be an astrophysicist, a scientist who studies all the objects in the universe, including planets, moons, comets, asteroids, stars, and the space in between.

As a schoolchild, Neil visited the Hayden Planetarium in New York City. He marveled at the show of the nighttime sky with the Milky Way and so many stars that he wondered if they were real. He decided to look at the sky himself. Neil began on his apartment-building rooftop with a pair of binoculars. The moon never had appeared so big, but he wanted to see more.

Neil received his first telescope from his parents in the seventh grade, when he was twelve years old. He could now see the planets and the stars, but he *still* wanted to see more.

Neil bought an even bigger telescope for himself with money he earned from walking dogs in his neighborhood. He also took classes on astronomy on his own at the planetarium. After ninth grade, Neil attended an astronomy camp in the Mojave Desert in California. He loved that campers were expected to stay up late at night to see planets, moons, stars, and galaxies. Viewing the constellation Scorpius was even more meaningful to campers who were trying to avoid the poison pincers of real scorpions on the ground during the day.

That same year, Neil ventured on an expedition to the coast of Africa to witness a total solar eclipse. The Explorers Club in New York City had awarded Neil a scholarship based on his class participation at the Hayden Planetarium.[1] Neil was the youngest person on the ship among scientists, engineers, and astronauts. At age fourteen, Neil's fate was set—he was determined to become a scientist who studied the universe.

Why Studying Space Is Important

Whether, like Neil, you plan a career studying the universe or you just enjoy studying the stars as a hobby, you also can explore the night sky from a rooftop. To start, maybe your backyard or a nearby park are better places. One dark night, lie in the grass away from the trees and bright lights. As the blades of grass tickle the backs of your knees and a mosquito buzzes near your ear, look at the stars and planets as they shine above you. Try to find the constellations, age-old patterns of stars outlining animals, people, and objects such as the Big Dipper. Or play your own game of connect the dots and design your personal constellation.

Neil as a thirteen-year-old. *(Courtesy of Neil deGrasse Tyson)*

If you have binoculars or a telescope, you will discover even more stars and will be able to see the planets close up. Then, you will be among the successful space scientists, such as Neil, exploring the universe.

It is human nature to explore not just our planet but also whatever is beyond it. We are curious creatures who always want to know more and figure things out. By looking at the stars, we have learned how the universe began, how stars are formed, and how our sun and planets came to be. By looking at planets, we may one day discover signs of life somewhere besides Earth. And by looking at galaxies, we may be able to predict the future of the universe.

We have learned so much already, but there are still many mysteries that will keep us looking farther and farther into space for a long time. We are fortunate to have clever brains and the imagination to wonder what is out there in space.

We Are Starstuff

> Not only do we live among the stars, the stars live within us.
> —Neil deGrasse Tyson, *Death by Black Hole*, 2007

Space scientists have determined the individual elements that make up stars. The elements from exploding stars found their way to Earth. This starstuff became a part of the molecules that make up all life on Earth, including our own human life. Neil says it best, "We are all connected; to each other biologically; to the earth, chemically; to the rest of the universe, atomically."[2] We look at the stars to learn more about ourselves and from where we came.

Today, Neil is an astrophysicist who looks at stars all the time.[3]

Since 1995, Neil has worked as the Frederick P. Rose Director of the Hayden Planetarium, the place where his dreams began. The planetarium is part of the American Museum of Natural History in Manhattan.[4] In addition to running the planetarium, Neil is responsible for the exhibits, programs for the public, and educational online resources. Let's find out how Neil arrived at his destination and learn about the universe along the way.

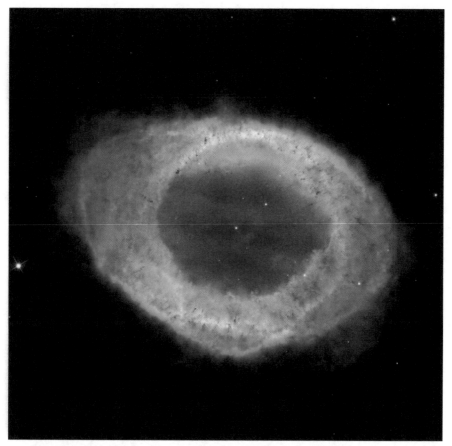

The Ring Nebula. A planetary nebula also known as M57 and NGC 6720. *(Image from NASA, ESA, and Robert O'Dell [Vanderbilt University])*

Chapter 2

A SPACE SCIENTIST GROWS UP

The universe called to me.

—Neil deGrasse Tyson,
interview with Roger Bingham, 2009

Childhood

Neil likes to tell people that he is the same age as the National Aeronautics and Space Administration (NASA). He was born on October 5, 1958, in New York City, just days after NASA was established.[1] Neil grew up in an apartment building in the Bronx, New York. The Tyson family, Neil, his two parents, a brother, and a sister, was comfortably middle-class.

He had a happy childhood during which his caring and supportive parents raised him. His father's mother (paternal grandmother), Altima deGrasse Tyson, lived with them for a while. Altima's maiden name, deGrasse, became the middle name of both Neil and his father. Neil is proud to use his middle name because he appreciates that his grandmother encouraged him to go to college and to do well in school.

Despite his grandmother's encouragement, Neil says that he was not a remarkable student in elementary school or high school.

Neil as a four-year-old child. *(Courtesy of Neil deGrasse Tyson)*

Most of his learning took place outside of school, such as during classes he enjoyed at the Hayden Planetarium. Still, Neil describes himself as a "nerdy kid," one who managed to earn high scores in mathematics, win science fairs, and join the physics club.

Seventh grade was Neil's favorite school year. His family moved to Lexington, Massachusetts, for his father's job. Neil's father, Cyril, worked for the mayor of New York City for many years. When Neil was eleven, Cyril took a break for a one-year appointment at Harvard University. That year, Neil achieved straight As, his best grades ever. On his twelfth birthday, his parents gave him his first telescope. Neil loved looking at the stars and the planets through the telescope in his backyard rather than with binoculars

Neil's high school yearbook photograph. *(Courtesy of Neil deGrasse Tyson)*

on a rooftop. By the time Neil was in eighth grade, when Cyril finished at Harvard, the Tyson family returned to the Bronx apartment building where Neil set up his new telescope on the roof.

Wrestling

Wrestling is a form of martial arts that is one of the world's oldest sports. It began as a form of combat thousands of years ago but soon became an athletic event in ancient Greece, Egypt, China, and Japan. Wrestling continues to this day as a competitive sport in high school, college, and the Olympics.

Wrestling is a match between two opponents, male or female, who are paired for age and weight. They perform within a large circle on a thick, rubber mat. The goal of wrestling is to pin your opponent's shoulders to the mat while trying to keep your opponent from pinning you. A wrestler has to learn hundreds of moves and holds, such as arm drags, bear hugs, and headlocks.

The main styles of wrestling are sumo, Greco-Roman, and freestyle. The collegiate wrestling that Neil did is known as folkstyle, which is similar to freestyle but with less body lifting and throwing down of your opponent on the mat. All styles of wrestling require strength, skill, and strategy. Each style depends on a referee to control the action, keep the match safe, and calculate the scoring to determine a winner.

The professional wrestling that is popular entertainment today started as a carnival sideshow. Although somewhat athletic, it is more of a presentation than a sport because it follows a dramatic script with a preplanned "winner."

The ancient Greek philosopher Plato was a wrestler who was good enough to compete in the Olympics. He believed that people should work toward a balance between physical training for the body and exercises of our minds and intellects. Neil's philosophy is similar. He enjoyed being an athlete and being in good shape physically while at the same time strengthening his mind through learning. In fact, Neil's knowledge of physics came in handy when he was practicing the forceful moves of wrestling.

Neil resumed taking classes at the Hayden Planetarium for the rest of junior high and high school. By high school, he was also enrolled in advanced mathematics and physics classes. During the last two years of high school, Neil participated in the sport of wrestling, and the wrestling team selected him to be captain in his senior year. Neil graduated from the Bronx High School of Science in 1976.

Growing Up in the 1960s

Neil was a child of the first generation said to be raised by the television. In the 1960s, before cable and satellite access existed, television had only a few channels and generally was in black and white. Computers at that time were so large that they filled an entire room and cost tens of thousands of dollars, so no one had one at home. But children did not care as much about TV and computers, as they spent hours each day playing with friends outside. Baseball fields were full of children playing pick-up games rather than organized league games. There were more mothers, like Sunchita, Neil's mother, who stayed at home to raise children, and neighbors watched out for each other's children.

The differences between 1960 and today are not all positive. Boys were unfairly favored over girls in education, sports, and future professions. Boys wanted to be firemen, policemen, and baseball players, while girls were encouraged to be nurses, school-teachers, and secretaries. Today, boys and girls have more similar opportunities for education and employment. Women can be fire-fighters and police officers; men can be secretaries and nurses. Sports in schools are more evenly offered to girls and boys now, but professional sport opportunities still are limited for women.

One of the areas in which change toward equal treatment has been positive is education. In the past, girls were not expected to excel in mathematics and science. Fortunately, that has changed and today both boys and girls and people of all races can study astronomy to be an astrophysicist.

Race in America

In the 1960s, America was in turmoil over a policy of segregation that separated blacks and whites in social, educational, and economic opportunities. African American citizens were forced to live in separate housing, go to separate schools, and work in separate jobs. Today, it is hard to imagine that black people were expected to use different public restrooms and eat in different restaurants than were white people.

Segregation was more of an open issue in the southern part of our country, especially when blacks were denied their right to vote. Martin Luther King Jr. (1929–1968) was a patriotic minister who believed in equality among the races and the right of all people to vote in our democracy. Dr. King began a nonviolent civil-rights movement. Neil's father, Cyril, actively was involved in civil rights during that time.

Sadly, some blacks were beaten and even killed for insisting on equal rights to vote, to receive a decent education, and to end forced segregation that made them second-class citizens. Certain narrow-minded groups of white people resisted these ideas. However, in 1964, President Lyndon Johnson signed an important civil-rights act to outlaw discrimination based on race and end segregation. In 1968, when Neil was not quite ten years old, Dr. King was assassinated. Our country still celebrates Dr. King's good work with a national holiday in his honor each January.

Neil was fortunate to grow up in the northern part of America, where he did not personally experience outright racial violence. He still felt some of the racial prejudices of our society, though. Neil long has been bothered that many whites regard blacks in general as less intelligent. Lower academic achievement arises because many black Americans were deprived of cultural-enrichment and educational opportunities. The actual intelligence of children is not related to race or the color of skin.

Neil benefited from a good educational environment and the enrichment Sunchita and Cyril provided. Growing up, Neil felt that he had to prove especially to other people that he was smart enough and qualified to be a scientist. Today, Neil has confidence in his ability to be accepted for who he is, a scientist who happens to be black. He no longer has to prove himself to other scientists, to white people, or to the world because of his race.

For a time, Neil struggled with whether he made the right decision to be a scientist instead of using his intelligence to work for racial equality. Then, after earning his PhD, Neil was asked to appear on television to answer questions about the sun. As he watched himself on TV later, he saw a scientist who was black speaking as an expert. Other than a very few athletes and actors, there were no blacks on TV when Neil grew up. Seeing himself as a scientific expert made Neil realize he had made the right career choice and served both interests.

People often wonder why Neil did not try to be an astronaut. In the 1960s, astronauts were all white men with crew cuts. There were no women or black astronauts. So Neil never thought of trying to be an astronaut. In 1961, a fourteen-year-old girl wrote a letter to NASA asking how she could become an astronaut. NASA responded that women were not allowed to be astronauts. That girl grew up to be Hillary Rodham Clinton, former First Lady and secretary of state for the United States. Hillary also went on to be a senator from New York and a presidential candidate. It was not until 1967 that NASA accepted its first black astronaut, and 1978 when it accepted its first woman.[2]

Mentors

Neil does not think that it is a good idea for anyone to view another person as a model to copy. To Neil, every person is unique and should develop his or her own talents. Still, he has been inspired by certain people whose traits or achievements are exceptional and meaningful to him. He prefers to call people he has learned from "mentors" rather than "role models."

Sunchita and Cyril

Neil credits his parents for stimulating much of his ambition and success. They did not know much about astronomy or science, but they always encouraged Neil to follow his interests, to learn, and to pursue his dreams. His father, Cyril deGrasse Tyson, was a sociologist, a specialist in the study of people in society. His mother, Sunchita Feliciano Tyson, stayed home to raise three children. After the children were grown, Sunchita returned to college for an advanced degree in gerontology, the study of elderly people.

Sunchita and Cyril instilled in Neil their family values for a love of learning and an appreciation of cultural opportunities. They introduced him to the Hayden Planetarium. When Neil was a child, his parents took him and his siblings to a different museum or cultural activity each weekend. They might go to the zoo or a sporting event one week, then attend the opera or a Broadway show the next. But it was the Hayden Planetarium that stayed with Neil and defined his life.

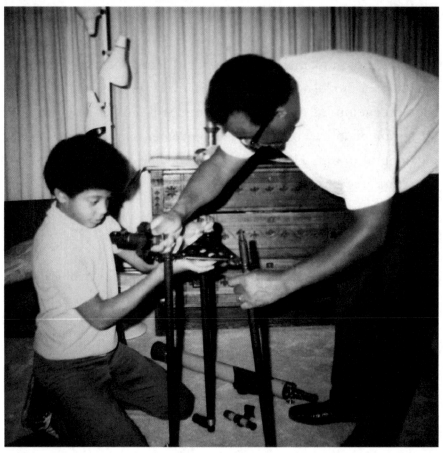

Neil's parents gave him his first telescope for his twelfth birthday. His father, Cyril, is helping Neil assemble the telescope. *(Courtesy of Neil deGrasse Tyson)*

Sir Isaac Newton (1643–1727)

Neil believes that Sir Isaac Newton was the smartest person who ever lived. Although he admires Newton's intellect, Neil hesitates to call Newton a role model. Newton was known as a difficult and disagreeable person. Neil has read everything Newton wrote, and he is happy to learn from Newton. But Neil does not want to be just like Newton.

Sir Isaac Newton (1643–1727). *(Used with permission from Shutter-stock/Georgios Kollidas)*

A favorite fable about Newton claims that he discovered gravity when an apple fell on his head. Actually, the apple did not strike him, but he did watch an apple fall and realize that the gravity forcing an apple to the ground is the same force that keeps the moon circling the earth. Newton is considered a great scientist because, in addition to describing gravity, he studied what light is made of, he developed an application of mathematics called calculus, and he defined the laws of motion. We will explore more about his accomplishments in chapter 3.

Other Scientists

There is no one scientist after whom Neil patterned his career or modeled himself. He prefers to select bits and pieces of the qualities he likes in others as a guide. A few scientists with admirable qualities who stand out in Neil's eyes are Fred Hess, Mark Chartrand III, and Carl Sagan.

Dr. Hess taught some of the classes Neil took at the Hayden Planetarium. Dr. Hess had an impressive voice and teaching style that influenced the way Neil lectures today. Dr. Chartrand, who also taught at the planetarium, incorporated humor into his lectures. Neil thought learning about space was fun, so he injects humor into his own work regularly, too.

Carl Sagan (1934–1996) is best known for popularizing interest in space study through his 1980 PBS television series, *Cosmos: A Personal Voyage*.[3] He was an accomplished astronomer, astrophysicist, and author. Neil had the good fortune to meet Dr. Sagan at Cornell University while Neil was still in high school. When Neil applied to colleges, he visited Cornell and found Dr. Sagan to be friendly, helpful, and caring. Neil now models his interactions with students after his meeting with Dr. Sagan.

Like Dr. Sagan, Neil enjoys writing books about the universe

Dr. Carl Sagan (1934–1996). *(Image © 1980 Druyan-Sagan Associates, Inc., by Eduardo Castaneda)*

that are accessible to the general public. Recently, Neil hosted the continuation of *Cosmos* with updated information for a new generation of television viewers. Neil commends Dr. Sagan for leading the way in public science education. Dr. Sagan took much grief from the scientific community for simplifying space for the benefit of nonscientists. Many of Dr. Sagan's colleagues thought that his effort to popularize space science lessened the status of their important work. Neil feels fortunate that he does not have to face that kind of criticism.

College

Neil knew he would go to college because his family assumed that he would. He applied to Harvard, the Massachusetts Institute of Technology (MIT), and Cornell, among others. Even after meeting Dr. Sagan at Cornell, Neil decided to attend Harvard, where he earned a bachelor of arts degree in physics in 1980.

College was not only about science and mathematics for Neil. He enjoyed humanities courses, including art, literature, and music. Neil continued wrestling and competed for the varsity team at Harvard. To his physical activities he also added dancing, even performing with two dance companies, and winning an award for Latin ballroom dancing. Neil also volunteered to tutor math for prisoners in a penitentiary, which he describes as an eye-opening yet rewarding experience.

After graduation from Harvard, Neil enrolled in graduate school at the University of Texas at Austin. He completed a master of arts degree in astronomy in 1983. To earn extra money while in grad school, Neil worked as a math tutor for undergraduates, which was quite a bit different from working with prisoners. Neil met his future wife, Alice Young, also a grad student, in a physics class they shared.

Neil started his doctorate at the University of Texas but later transferred to Columbia University in New York City. He graduated with a doctorate in astrophysics in 1991.

Neil still would like to go into space someday, out beyond the moon, which is the farthest that any astronauts have gone so far. But this is not a book about being an astronaut and going into space, it is about becoming a space scientist and studying about the stars.

Hubble Ultra Deep Field, 2014. This image shows over ten thousand galaxies using light ranging from ultraviolet to near-infrared. *(Image from NASA, ESA, H. Teplitz and M. Rafelski [IPAC/Caltech], A. Koeke-moer [STScI], R. Windhorst [ASU], and Z. Levay [STScI])*

Chapter 3

LOOKING AT ALL BEAUTIFUL THINGS

What could be more beautiful than the heavens, which contain all beautiful things?

—Nicolaus Copernicus,
On the Revolutions of the Heavenly Spheres, 1543

Since our early ancestors slept outside their caves two hundred thousand years ago and wondered about the twinkling lights moving across the night sky, humans have been astronomers at heart. Astronomy is the study of space and everything in it. Space scientists study planets, moons, stars, galaxies, and the space between them.

BEFORE THE TELESCOPE

Ancient Times

As far back as 2,500 years ago, the ancient Greeks were the first people to try to understand the physics of the universe in order to explain things in the sky. Tales of earlier ancient Babylonian and Egyptian civilizations influenced them. The famous Greek philosopher Aristotle (384 BCE–322 BCE), was the first to study the nature of the universe as science and write scientific laws based on his observations.

Aristotle thought that Earth was made of four elements—earth, air, fire, and water. The "heavenly bodies," as he called them, were not like Earth. They were made of a fifth element, aether, which was perfect, shiny, and unchanging. Aristotle determined that Earth was round and that it did not move. Instead, all the planets and stars, including the sun, moved in a circle around Earth. Other astronomers did not challenge Aristotle's laws of the universe for 1,500 years.

Today we still know many stars and constellations by their original Greek names, such as the Dog Star, Sirius, and the constellation Orion. Our word *planet* comes from the Greek word for "wanderer." The Greeks saw that the planets wandered across the sky while the stars stayed in the same place relative to each other.

Five hundred years after Aristotle, an Egyptian astronomer named Ptolemy (90 CE–168 CE) tried to explain the orbits of the solar system using mathematical terms and circles. He left Earth at the center of the universe. Ptolemy attempted to count the stars, listing over one thousand stars and naming many of the constellations they form.

Renaissance Science

Not much new happened by way of scientific study of objects in the sky from ancient times until the period known as the Renaissance (which lasted from the fourteenth to the seventeenth century), a time when learning regained importance. Nicolaus Copernicus

(1473– 1543) was the first scientist to seriously question Aristotle's laws of the universe. Copernicus lived in Poland during the Renaissance. He reasoned that the sun is the center of the solar system instead of the earth. That way, the motion of the other planets made sense. Copernicus was correct about the solar system. Unfortunately, he thought that the sun was the center of the universe, too. In chapter 4, we will find out why he was wrong about that.

Thinkers of his time rejected Copernicus's theory of the sun in the center of the solar system. To them, it was common sense that Earth was not moving and Copernicus had no convincing evidence to prove otherwise. Most important, the powerful Roman Catholic Church rejected the findings of Copernicus. The church adopted Aristotle's "natural and divine order" with the earth in the center of the universe.

After Copernicus died, a Danish astronomer named Tycho Brahe (1546–1601) tried to determine the distance to the stars. He built special instruments to measure the positions of planets and stars as they moved in the sky. Brahe estimated the distance to stars, but he was not close to their actual distance. Astronomers would not figure out the distance to the stars for several hundred more years. Still, Brahe's measurements of the stars showing that they moved and changed proved that at least one of Aristotle's laws was wrong—heavenly bodies are not perfect. Brahe's data and conclusions would prove invaluable to future scientists.

Perhaps more excellent things will be discovered in time, either by me or by others, with the help of a similar instrument.
—Galileo Galilei, *Sidereus Nuncius*, 1610

THE TELESCOPE REVOLUTION

In the early 1600s, the great Italian thinker Galileo Galilei (1564–1642) heard about a spyglass that made distant objects look closer. Galileo obtained a spyglass that he improved to make images larger and clearer. When he turned it to the sky to look at the moon and the planets, Galileo's spyglass became the first telescope.

With the aid of his telescope, Galileo discovered that Jupiter had four moons that he could see—Io, Europa, Ganymede, and Callisto—that we now call the Galilean moons. Galileo also studied our own moon. He was amazed to find mountains and craters on its surface. Aristotle was wrong about heavenly bodies being smooth and perfect. Perhaps Aristotle also was wrong about the sun and other planets circling Earth. When Galileo used his telescope to study the phases of Venus, he found evidence that Venus circles the sun, thereby proving that Copernicus was correct about the sun, *not* the earth, being the center of the solar system.

While Galileo worked in Italy, he wrote to another scientist in Poland named Johannes Kepler (1571–1630), who was a student of Tycho Brahe. When Brahe died, Kepler took over all of Brahe's astronomical measuring instruments and his years of accumulated data. Thanks to Galileo, Kepler was able to add the telescope to his toolkit. Kepler analyzed precise measurements of the movements of the planets, discovering that their orbits were not circular but elliptical (oval-shaped). Kepler's findings verified Copernicus's theory about the relationship between the sun and the planets. The data fit perfectly.

While Kepler figured out that the planets moved in elliptical orbits, it was left to Sir Isaac Newton to discover why. In 1687,

Newton explained that every object in the universe attracts all the other objects. The strength of the force of this gravity between objects depends on the size of the objects and the distance between them. Newton developed this realization into the laws of planetary motion. Newton's laws explained the mechanics that governed what those before him had observed.

Twentieth-Century Developments

The twentieth century witnessed an increase in knowledge about our universe. Early in the 1900s, a German-born physicist named Albert Einstein (1879–1955) replaced Newton's laws with a more sophisticated and accurate explanation of the mechanics of the universe. Einstein was not an astronomer, but he developed a general theory of relativity that explained better than Newton how objects move in space. Einstein theorized that space and time are curved by the energy of gravity and the mass of objects. The heavier an object is, the more space and time curve around it. The sun, which is larger than the earth, curves space and time more than earth. This curving of space-time is responsible for the motion of the planets around the sun, the motion of light through space, and the mechanics of the entire universe.

An American astronomer, Edwin Hubble (1889–1953), proved Einstein's theory of space being curved by gravity. Hubble was the first scientist to show that our universe is expanding, moving as Einstein predicted it would.[1]

Before Hubble, scientists believed that the galaxy in which we live, the Milky Way, was the only galaxy in space. Hubble showed that what was called the Andromeda Nebula was actually another galaxy. He went on to find thousands of additional galaxies. Hubble designed a system to classify galaxies by their shape. We still sort galaxies according to his system, whether they are spiral, elliptical, barred, regular, or irregular. Galaxies will be explained in more detail in chapter 4. The Hubble Space Telescope was named in Edwin Hubble's honor.

Not all accomplished astronomers of the past were male. An American woman astronomer was instrumental in helping Hubble ascertain that the Milky Way is not the only galaxy in the universe, as was commonly thought at the time. Henrietta Swan Leavitt (1868–1921) discovered that certain stars could be used to measure the distance between objects in space. Variable stars, called Cepheids, become brighter then dimmer at regular intervals. Leavitt calculated the distance from one Cepheid to another by studying their brightnesses. Leavitt's work was instrumental to Hubble in proving that the universe has many galaxies.[2]

> If I have seen farther, it is by standing on the shoulders of giants.[3]
>
> —Sir Isaac Newton, 1676

Neil agrees with Newton that scientists living today should appreciate the outstanding minds that came before them. Knowing that he is one scientist among many keeps Neil humble. Neil shares a special kindredship with Galileo and those who followed after him when he looks through a telescope as Galileo did long ago. What those who went before taught is the platform upon which Neil stands as he looks for more that he can add to the body of human knowledge about space.

On a public radio show several years ago, Neil was asked what he would want to have with him if he were stranded on a desert island. In addition to a case of his favorite wine, candles to write by, and music, Neil selected two books. The first was *Almagest*, written by Ptolemy in 150 CE, and the second was *Principia Mathematica*, written by Sir Isaac Newton in 1687. Of course, he also would want a telescope. Neil recommends that everyone own a telescope to develop a personal connection to the universe. Armed with a telescope and the shared learning of those who went before, a castaway could keep himself very busy indeed.

TOOLS OF A SPACE SCIENTIST– TELESCOPES AND LIGHT WAVES

Everyone has seen the moon and the stars. But have you really looked closely at the moon and the stars? With a telescope and the right light conditions, you can observe the moons of Jupiter as Galileo did. Tools help us expand our five senses to taste, smell, see, hear, and feel our world better and learn more. Telescopes are the tools that allow scientists to see farther into space than our eyes alone can take us.

Before we had telescopes, people often looked at new objects in space with fear and dread. A comet or an eclipse could be a warning that something bad was about to happen. But the telescope let people understand more about the actual objects in space and wonder what secrets nature was hiding in the dark. Many things in space we look at on purpose, but telescopes also expose things that we never knew were present in our universe.

Galileo's first telescope was just a lead tube spyglass with two lenses in it. A lens is a disc of glass that has been shaped and polished to magnify and focus objects. Later, scientists cut lenses to make them bigger and more powerful, until Sir Isaac Newton designed a telescope that let in even more light with sharper images using mirrors instead of lenses. Today's telescopes with glass lenses are called *refractors*, and those with mirrors are called *reflecting telescopes*. Many telescopes combine lenses and mirrors to create an image.

As telescopes continue to be made bigger to increase magnification, astronomers see even deeper into space. Scientists are solving some of the mysteries of the universe such as how stars evolve, how far it is to other galaxies, and how old our solar system is.

Light

Physicists know that light is made of photons that are both particles and waves. A photon is the basic particle of light energy found in all wavelengths that travels at the speed of light. Nothing travels faster than light at 186,282 miles per second (299,792 kilometers per second). Although how light can be both particle and wave is a story worth telling, it is beyond the scope of this book.

At certain wavelengths, the waves and particles that make up light are visible to our eyes. Meanwhile, at wavelengths above and below our vision level, light still flows through the universe, though we cannot see it all.

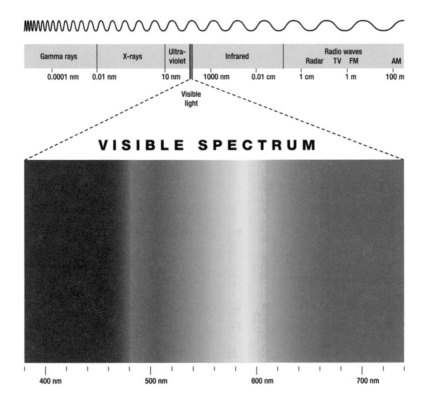

Electromagnetic Light Spectrum. *(Used with permission from Shutterstock/Peter Hermes Furian)*

Visible Light

Visible light has been apparent to humans since the beginning of time. Without using any instruments, that is how we see the sun and all things around us.

Even though light travels so fast, it takes eight minutes for a photon leaving the sun to reach the earth. We use the speed of light as a measure for large distances.

The distance from the sun to Earth is about 93 million miles

(150 million kilometers). This measurement is called an astronomical unit (AU) and is used to measure distances in our solar system. For instance, Jupiter is 5 AU from the sun (483 million miles or 780 million kilometers). Dwarf planet Pluto is very far away, at 40 AU from the sun (3,666 million miles or 5,913 million kilometers).

We also use light to measure distances that are vaster than the expanse between planets. While the edge of our solar system is extremely far away, the closest stars are even farther. Outside the solar system, great distances are measured in light-years. A light-year is the distance that light travels in one year, or about 6 trillion miles (10 trillion kilometers). The closest star to Earth is Proxima Centauri. It is 4 light-years from us. That means the starlight we see today left the star four years ago and traveled 24 trillion miles (39 trillion kilometers) to reach us.

In 1672, Newton discovered that visible light, when passed through a prism (a triangular wedge of glass), breaks into individual colors called a *spectrum*. The spectrum shows the colors of the rainbow—red, orange, yellow, green, blue, and violet (indigo is considered a shade of blue). This spectrum is in order from the longest light wave of red to the shortest, violet. Scientists know that starlight breaks into the same spectrum as sunlight.

Astrophysicists use a device called a spectrograph to collect starlight through a telescope and break up the light waves with a prism. The different colors that the light breaks into tell scientists the temperature and chemical makeup of the star, as well as how it is rotating and how fast it is moving. The light waves from a star also reveal whether it is moving toward or away from Earth. An object getting closer to Earth has shorter wavelengths, so its light is shifted to the blue end of the spectrum. This is called *blue shift*. An object moving away has longer wavelengths toward the red end of the spectrum; this is called *red shift.*

Light Waves outside the Visible Spectrum

Galileo and Newton used telescopes that could collect only the light we can see with our eyes. Since then, astrophysicists have learned that even more invisible light exists than does visible light. Invisible light is made of photons and waves that operate at wavelengths below and above our vision level. Different stars shine in visible light and invisible light in other wavelengths. The other forms of light in the universe that are considered invisible are: radio waves, microwaves, infrared light, ultraviolet light, x-rays, and gamma rays. Space scientists have developed special telescopes that collect the invisible light and translate it so we can "see" it for analysis and understanding.

The lowest-energy waves of invisible light below our vision are radio waves. These are harmless waves that transmit sound and images, which scientists discovered in the late 1800s. Next are microwaves, which are made of the same energy that cooks food in microwave ovens and that operates speed radar guns for the police. Infrared light is next in energy level or wavelength. We use this light to keep food warm and to look for sources of heat through special tools, such as night-vision goggles that are used to find a warm body in the dark.

Above the visible spectrum are additional light waves. The first in higher energy is ultraviolet (UV) light. UV light from the sun can burn our skin and cause cancer. That is why we apply sunscreen to keep our skin from burning. UV also produces the glowing black-light effect we sometimes see in dark rooms.

Next are x-ray waves, which are the same as those used to take x-rays of our bones. We use them to "see" our bones through our flesh. X-rays are helpful in this regard, but they also can cause cancer. The strongest and most harmful light waves if they strike us directly are gamma rays. Fortunately, on Earth, a layer of ozone in the atmosphere protects us from most of the danger that ultraviolet, x-ray, and gamma-ray waves bring from space.

These invisible forms of light carry information about space to Earth. Space scientists use telescopes that can measure and analyze each form of light, not just visible, so we can learn even more about objects in space than Galileo or Newton ever did. Certain telescopes measure gamma rays from supernovae and black holes. NASA's Chandra X-ray Observatory, which is in outer space above our atmosphere, searches for x-rays from clusters of galaxies. Other telescopes measure infrared and microwave radiation from different parts of the sky.

Edwin Hubble's Legacy

After discovering that there were other galaxies, Edwin Hubble realized that the light from these galaxies was red shifted. He knew that meant the other galaxies were moving away from us. Therefore, the universe was expanding. Hubble also concluded that the farther away a galaxy is, the faster it is moving. The telescope that Hubble used in the 1920s was at the top of Mount Wilson in Pasadena, California.

Neil says the best place to observe photons in the night sky is from a mountain top in the clear air away from bright city lights. He has looked through telescopes on the mountains of New Mexico,

Texas, Arizona, and the Andes in Chile, South America. A famous place to observe the night sky is the from the Keck telescopes that sit atop the dormant volcano Mauna Kea in Hawaii.

The Hubble Space Telescope in orbit around Earth. *(Image from NASA)*

New York City is one of the worst places to look through a telescope, according to Neil. The city is a victim of light pollution, too much wasted light that shines up into the sky instead of down on the ground. As a result, it is difficult to see true darkness and experience the full range of stars. On a very dark night, we can see portions of our own Milky Way galaxy. However, because of artificial light, most people in the United States cannot view the Milky Way from where they live.

Telescopes at the top of Kitt Peak in Arizona. *(Image by the author)*

To overcome both light pollution and the bending of light in Earth's atmosphere, astronomers decided to launch telescopes into space. We have moved above the Earth's atmosphere to search. There are many telescopes up there, but the most famous one is the Hubble Space Telescope (HST), named after Edwin Hubble. The HST collects beautiful images in the visible light spectrum. HST sends amazing images back to Earth, including pictures of ancient galaxies that began shining millions of years ago. Just as Hubble changed thinking about galaxies, so now do many of the discoveries of the HST revise what we understand about our universe.

Other Tools

Space scientists use tools and knowledge beyond the measurement of visible and invisible light obtained through telescopes to do their work. The periodic table of elements is a useful tool. This is a chart of boxes for all known 118 elements, of which 98 occur naturally in the universe and the rest are made in laboratories. Elements that have similar characteristics are grouped together, such as gases, liquids, and metals. The table also indicates how the elements interact with each other. Scientists since Newton's time have figured out that every element on the periodic table, when heated, shows its own individual color. A spectrometer attached to a telescope breaks down light into colors. By analyzing the colors of objects in space, astrophysicists learn the chemical makeup of stars and the atmospheres of planets that orbit them. Advances in chemistry have enabled astronomers to measure and assess the elements in the stars and galaxies.

Computers have become useful tools for astrophysicists, too. Scientists are constantly making bigger and better telescopes that are able to catch every photon of light in space. Before computers became available to set the direction of the telescopes, gather images, and evaluate information, scientists had to do that work by hand. Now computers are programmed to take over the time-consuming work. Computers also convert the light collected by a telescope into digital data that can be easily compared and analyzed for patterns. Moreover, the colors and light in images may be enhanced by computers to see things that were not in our visual range.

Finally, scientists compile and store digital information about space in computers where scientists from around the world can view and use it. Astrophysicists expect to look at the sky for millions of objects in all light wavelengths and make a list of them. They created a huge database of astronomy that will serve as an additional tool for space exploration. Astrophysicists now spend less time looking through telescopes and more time sitting in front of computer screens.

ASTROPHYSICS AS A PROFESSION

Years ago, most space scientists were either astronomers or astrophysicists. Astronomers found and described objects in space, while astrophysicists worked to understand and explain the physical qualities of those objects. Today, Neil says that all professional astronomers are basically astrophysicists, so the terms are used interchangeably. Neil thinks that he has the "coolest job" as an astrophysicist because he is paid to look at and contemplate all of the beautiful things in the universe.

An astrophysicist needs to be good at science and mathematics. According to Neil, mathematics is the language of the universe, so you can talk to the universe if you know the right equations. As Neil put it, "While the world's nations speak different languages, everybody's mathematics looks the same."[4] Measuring and assessing the brightness, temperature, distance, and chemical composition of objects in the universe also requires knowledge of chemistry and physics. For example, astrophysicists must know the color signatures of elements. As much as astrophysicists might

Neil under the shadow of Saturn at the Hayden Planetarium. *(Image © 2014 Dan Deitch)*

want to visit the stars to check their temperatures, the technology does not yet exist for them to do so. Therefore, they must be skilled at reading the colors of the various spectrums of light collected from the stars.

Most science today is interdisciplinary, that is, it is based on a collaboration of different scientists from various fields. Astrophysicists work with scientists from related fields such as chemistry, physics, and geology. They might assist engineers to design the cameras and equipment in space telescopes so we can enjoy amazing images of galaxies. Or they may work with astrobiologists, who are scientists looking for signs of life outside our planet. Another scientist, called a cosmologist, is concerned with the cosmos or universe as a whole—how it came to be and how it evolves.

Becoming an astrophysicist requires one to study for many years. A student who wants to be an astrophysicist should consider working on obtaining a physics degree in college. Some universities also offer undergraduate degrees in astronomy and space science. Most astrophysicists then work on advanced degrees with a concentration in some aspect of space science. Astrophysicists can specialize in studying the formation of stars, comets, or black holes. They can also choose to search for planets outside our solar system or for the oldest galaxy in the universe. To become qualified for high-level work and accomplished in space science, one should earn a doctoral-level degree (a PhD).

An astrophysicist should have good communication skills. In addition to looking for stars and planets, astrophysicists have other jobs to do. Some enjoy teaching young scientists or educating the public about space through presentations, articles, and Internet postings. Among professionals, it is important to be able to write well so that new findings are related to other people. Also, some astrophysicists are active in writing blogs and managing websites. Indeed, particularly skilled communicators, such as Neil, are in charge of planetariums and observatories at the same time that they work as astrophysicists. Conveying enthusiasm about this exciting field and informing others about our place in the universe are rewarding parts of being an astrophysicist.

This is a good time to turn to the universe and learn about space and the objects that astrophysicists explore.

The Orion Nebula (also known as M42 and NGC 1976) is a massive nursery for newborn stars. *(Image from NASA, ESA, T. Megeath [University of Toledo], and M. Robberto [STScI])*

Chapter 4

THE EVOLUTION OF NEIL'S FAVORITE UNIVERSE

> Modern humans are not the first group of people to speculate about cosmic evolution, but we are the first to use the tools of science to describe the birth of the cosmos, trace its progress, and understand our place in it.
> —Neil deGrasse Tyson, *My Favorite Universe*, 2003

A BIG BANG BEGINNING

Edwin Hubble's discovery that the universe is expanding made scientists realize that the universe must have been much smaller at one time. Space scientists began looking backward in time to figure out the point at which the universe started.

About 14 billion years ago, our universe was compressed into a tiny area the size of a head of a pin. The energy in that speck was so extremely high, and the temperature so incredibly hot, that within seconds it expanded rapidly to the size of a beach ball. That ball rapidly cooled and expanded until it formed all the space, time, matter, and energy that make up the universe today. This theory of rapid expansion, or inflation, now is called the *big bang*.

While the energy of the baby universe was spreading, the temperature dropped dramatically. Small particles of energy joined to form atoms, the smallest units of elements. The first elements formed were the lightest gases—hydrogen (H) and helium (He). These gases were later to become the fuel for the birth of stars.

At the same time that the first gases formed, the released energy from the inflation created the first basic units of light called photons. These photons are now in the microwave part of the light spectrum described earlier. Astrophysicists detected ancient photons that make up a hot-light region of space, known as the cosmic microwave background (CMB), left over from shortly after the big bang. By measuring the CMB at the edge of the known universe, scientists determined the exact age of the universe to be 13.8 billion years old!

Neil is confident that the universe began with the big bang. His specialty in astrophysics is galaxy formation and stellar evolution. The evolution of the universe is more than how many stars are in the sky or how far away they are. Neil studied how new stars form, how old stars collapse and die, how stars accumulate into galaxies, and how black holes are involved in forming galaxies. Neil still wonders why the big bang happened and what existed before the universe. For now, those wonderings will have to remain mysteries of the evolution of the universe.

The Birth of Stars

Look up at the night sky and pick a special bright star, not just one to make a wish on, but one about which to wonder and learn. The photon of light entering your eye from that star traveled hundreds of light-years to delight you with its starshine. How did that star get up in the sky?

After the big bang, the brand-new universe was a hot cloud of gas. As the cosmic cloud cooled, atoms of hydrogen combined to form molecules. The first stars formed from these molecules of hydrogen and atoms of helium. It took over 100 million years for the gas to accumulate enough material to form the first stars. These early stars formed heavier elements in their nuclear furnaces and spread them out into space. The heavier elements combined and clumped together into larger particles, called dust. Space dust is tiny grains of material that become the building blocks for larger space objects.

Gravity holds together the gases in each star. When a star grows big enough, the pressure and temperature rise at its center. At about 27 million degrees Fahrenheit (15 million degrees Celsius), a thermonuclear reaction takes place. Thermonuclear fusion is the releasing of energy by combining small atoms to form larger ones, which happens only in the presence of high temperatures. The nuclei of hydrogen atoms fuse into atoms of helium in an explosion of energy released as heat and light. Planets and other space objects, such as asteroids, are not big enough to have that much pressure in their cores, so they do not give off light. The light you see from a planet is only light reflected off its surface by its star.

A star is basically a clump of fusing gases giving off light. Stars form in many sizes and fuse atoms at different temperatures. The largest stars are the hottest, and they appear white or blue. They tend to burn out quicker than the cooler, smaller stars that we see as yellow or red. Small stars continue fusing hydrogen into helium all their lives. Medium stars, like our sun, eventually convert helium into carbon, nitrogen, and oxygen. The largest stars do that, too. But then the massive stars, with their hotter centers up to 180 million degrees Fahrenheit (100 million degrees Celsius), fuse carbon, nitrogen, and oxygen to form other elements, such as sodium, magnesium, sulfur, calcium, all the way up to iron on the periodic table.

Stars may burn for billions of years before they run out of fuel. A space scientist could not live long enough to see a star's life. Fortunately, stars at all stages of life are available for astrophysicists to study. Just as people are born, live their lives, and die, so do stars. But unlike people, when stars die, they send their elements out into space to be reused in making new stars.

The periodic table of elements. *(Image from WPClip Art)*

Some large stars expand as they run out of fuel and turn red as they cool. These are called "red giants." When a red giant has finished fusing all of its helium, it will evolve and shrink into a "white dwarf." Smaller stars also shrink into white dwarfs as they die. The largest stars that explode as they are dying are called "supernovae." The energy of the supernova explosion is so great that elements heavier than iron result. All the new elements are blasted into space and settle into clouds of gas and dust, called "nebulae," where they are reused to make new stars. Nebulae are special so they need special consideration.

Nebulae

The Orion Nebula (M42) is a glowing cloud of gas and dust visible in our night sky. The energy of all the infant stars growing within light it up brightly.

Though they share a similar name, a nebula where baby stars are born is not the same as a "planetary nebula." Following the death of a star or a supernova explosion, the gas left from the outer layer of the star forms a shell around the dead star. This shell of gas spreads out slowly into space. The so-called planetary nebula is a beautiful image that has nothing to do with planets.

On July 4, 1054, Chinese astronomers witnessed a supernova so bright that it was visible in daylight. Later, scientists with telescopes thought the planetary nebula around this same supernova looked like a familiar sea creature, so they named it the Crab Nebula (M1). Other scientists studying the Crab Nebula discovered that what was left of the exploding star developed into a neutron star.

Neil says that neutron stars are his favorite objects in space because they are the densest celestial bodies. After a supernova explosion, the neutron parts of any remaining atoms cram together into a very small area. The density of a neutron star is as if the mass of our sun was squeezed into an area the size of a city. Sometimes neutron stars spin rapidly and send out streams of light. The Crab Nebula's neutron star is one of those. The motion of spinning light is known as a pulsar and resembles the beacon of a lighthouse. The pulsar in the Crab Nebula flashes an amazing thirty times a second. Neutron stars are so packed together by high gravity that they spin incredibly fast without flying apart into tiny pieces.

The Crab Nebula is a planetary nebula also known as NGC 1952.
(Image from NASA, ESA, and J. Hester and A. Loll [ASU])

Astrophysicists now know that the Crab Nebula is 6,300 light-years away from Earth. Because it is so far away, it is hard to see in the sky except with binoculars or a telescope. Look for it in the constellation Taurus.

Constellations

Ancient stargazers thought a particular pattern of stars looked like the head of a bull. That became the constellation Taurus, Latin for "bull." The Orion Nebula, where new stars are born, is found near the constellation Orion, which is named after a great Greek hunter. It is well known for the row of three stars indicating Orion's Belt. Both constellations Orion and Taurus are in the Northern Hemisphere. Constellations do move gradually across the night sky as the seasons change. But Orion's Belt always points directly to the head of the bull.

Some patterns of stars are part of the same cluster of stars. For example, the Pleiades (PLEE-a-deez), also called the Seven Sisters, are seven stars born from the Orion Nebula that have stayed together. Still, the stars we see in many other constellations are not all in the same group. The brightness of a star depends on its size, age, and how hot it is burning, not just its distance from Earth. Very bright stars can be far away, while dimmer ones can be closer.

Over time, astronomers arranged the night sky into eighty-eight constellations. These are named primarily for the Greek and Roman figures that the ancient people imagined. Far in the past, the constellations were used for navigation. Ship captains used the night sky as a map with familiar shapes such as Orion pointing the way. Today, we use the constellations as maps for locating particular stars. You are probably familiar with the seven stars of the Big Dipper, part of the constellation Ursa Major, the Great Bear. Did you know the star at the end of the Little Dipper is Polaris, the North Star?

Constellations in the Northern Hemisphere are not the same as those below the Equator in the Southern Hemisphere. The people of Canada view a night sky with different star patterns than do people who live in Australia. Regardless of which constellations we see each night, we can enjoy many of the eighty-eight amazing constellations that are in our Milky Way galaxy.[1]

The brightest star we see from Earth is Sirius (the Dog Star). It is 8.8 light-years away and appears in the constellation Canis Major (the Greater Dog). Its light takes longer than eight years to travel 52 trillion miles (83 trillion kilometers) to reach us. Most stars in the sky are not actually solitary stars.

More than half of all stars are binary, that is, made of two stars orbiting each other. Neil's favorite star is Albireo, in the head of the swan constellation, Cygnus. It is not the brightest star in the constellation, but a close look through a telescope shows that it is a binary star. One star is a hot blue color and the other is a cooler gold. They are as beautiful as looking at a sapphire and a topaz gem next to each other. Albireo is extremely far from Earth at 430 light-years away. The closest stars to Earth (after the sun) are the binary Alpha Centauri (A and B) at 4.3 light-years away (25 trillion miles, 41 trillion kilometers) and nearby Proxima Centauri at 4.2 light-years.

Galaxies

Gravity pulls stars together into groups called galaxies. In the universe, there are at least 100 billion galaxies, each containing

How Are Celestial Bodies Named?

While constellations were named for the objects that ancient observers saw in their star patterns, planets were given the names of Greek and Roman mythological gods and goddesses. Many of the individual stars, such as Albireo, were named by medieval Arabian astronomers. Comets and asteroids frequently are named for or by their discoverers. Galaxies and nebulae often are named for the object they most resemble, like the Sombrero galaxy or the Butterfly Nebula.

Some well-known objects, such as the Andromeda galaxy, carry several names. In addition to its popular name Andromeda, our neighbor galaxy also is known as NGC 224 and M31. "NGC" refers to the *New General Catalog* and the "M" stands for Messier. In the 1700s, Charles Messier hunted the night sky with his telescope, looking for comets. He found many other bright and beautiful objects, mainly nebulae, star clusters, and galaxies. Messier created a list of 110 objects that he numbered M1 to M110.[2]

Then in the 1800s, a brother-and-sister team, William and Caroline Herschel, added more space objects to Messier's list in their *New General Catalog*. The Herschels discovered almost 2,500 objects; of these, 110 were Messier's. The objects on both lists have two numbers. William was the astronomer who discovered Uranus (YOOR-ah-nus). Caroline found nine comets and many nebulae. Space scientists have added more objects to the NGC since the Herschels' time. Today the NGC lists almost eight thousand celestial bodies.

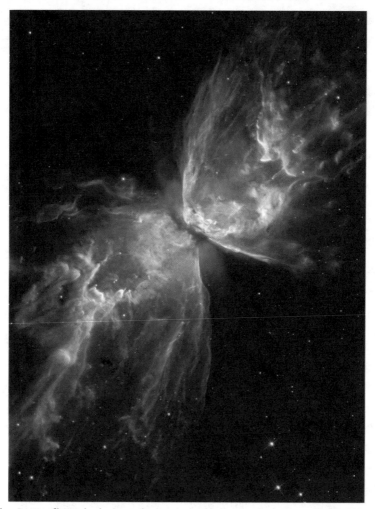

The Butterfly Nebula is a planetary nebula also known as NGC 6302.
(Image from NASA, ESA, and the Hubble SM4 ERO Team)

hundreds of billions of stars. It is hard for our minds to comprehend how large a number of stars there are.

To this day, we use Edwin Hubble's category of galaxies. Hubble learned that galaxies form into three distinct shapes. About two-thirds of the known galaxies are spirals; these are primarily young galaxies, and they include our Milky Way and our next-door neighbor Andromeda. The second shape found in older galaxies is called *elliptical* because these galaxies have no arms and are oval-shaped. Elliptical galaxies look like footballs. Most of their gas formed into stars a long time ago. Irregular galaxies with no particular shape are the third galaxy type. Irregular galaxies often form after two galaxies collide.

The spiral Pinwheel galaxy is also called M101 and NGC 5457. *(Image from NASA, ESA, K. Kuntz [JHU], F. Bresolin [University of Hawaii], J. Trauger [JPL], J. Mould [NOAO], Y. H. Chu [University of Illinois, Urbana], and STScI)*

The stars in galaxies are very far apart from each other. Neil explains that when galaxies collide, the stars do not crash into one another. Stars will be affected by other stars' gravity and may be pushed or pulled around. Mainly the gas and dust among the stars will move and spread, creating the interesting shapes of colliding galaxies. For instance, Neil loves the long, wispy tails that formed from the collision of the Mice galaxies (NGC 4676).

An elliptical galaxy, NGC 1132. *(Image from NASA, ESA, and the Hubble Heritage [STScI/AURA] Collaboration)*

Most galaxy collisions took place when the universe was only three billion years old. That was the peak time of galaxy building. The universe was smaller then, and more gases collided to make stars. Few new galaxies are being made today, although there are still many established nebulae making new stars.

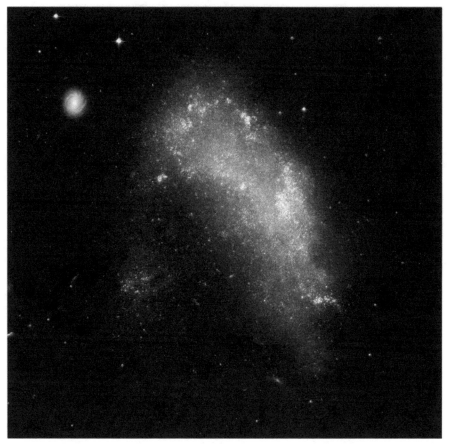

An irregular galaxy, NGC 1427A. *(NASA, ESA, and the Hubble Heritage Team [Image from STScI/AURA])*

Galaxies are not spread evenly throughout the universe. There are huge empty spaces called *cosmic voids*. While most of space is empty of observable matter, scientists know that an invisible substance and an invisible force control the growth of the cosmos. The substance is called *dark matter*, and the force is called *dark energy*.

Although we do not fully understand either, both are essential to explain the evolution of our universe.

The Mice—interacting galaxies (NGC 4676) shows two galaxies colliding. *(Image from NASA, H. Ford [JHU], G. Illingworth [UCSC/LO], M. Clampin [STScI], G. Hartig [STScI], the ACS Science Team, and ESA)*

Dark Matter

When the big bang began our universe, it produced a mysterious particle called dark matter. Particles of dark matter do not give off light and do not interact with regular matter, such as the stuff of which you are made. It is invisible to our eyes and our instruments for now; so scientists are building detectors that will enable us to "see" dark matter in the future.

But scientists know that dark matter exists because it has both gravity and an effect on matter around it. In fact, clumps of dark matter may be what hold galaxies together. Dark matter exerts so much gravity that astrophysicists calculate 90 percent of total matter in the universe is dark, while the remaining 10 percent is ordinary matter that we can see.

Dark Energy

Scientists are also developing detectors for dark energy, a mysterious force that causes the expansion of the universe to accelerate. In the early universe after the big bang, young galaxies were close together until dark energy acted against gravity to force the galaxies to move farther away from each other. As the universe spreads out, the antigravity pressure of dark energy increases and carries galaxies farther out with it. Astrophysicists have determined that dark energy is pulling galaxies apart at a rate that keeps getting faster.[3]

Black Holes

When Neil meets people in public, he is generally asked three questions: (1) Did the big bang really happen? (2) Do black holes exist? and (3) Is there life in other parts of the universe? We answered the first question earlier, and life elsewhere will be addressed in chapter 9. Here, Neil answers the question about black holes.

When gravity crushes a giant star and causes it to collapse in on itself, a black hole is formed. The gravity is so strong that even light, the fastest thing we know, cannot escape. Because light does not get out, the hole is called "black." A black hole takes the shape of a spinning funnel. The wide edge of the funnel is the *event horizon*, where space and time are curved by being pulled into the singularity, or the center, of the funnel.

Illustration of a black hole showing the spinning event horizon and the central singularity. *(Used with permission from Shutterstock/ Catmando)*

Black holes grow larger by pulling star and galaxy material along the event horizon and into the singularity. When a star gets too close to the event horizon, the black hole will swallow it. As the star nears the singularity, the intense gravity of the black hole shreds the star to pieces, causing it to release a large amount of heat and light. Neil delights in describing what would happen to a person being pulled into a black hole feet-first. The pull of the gravity would stretch the body and snap the body in half at the waist. Then with pieces continuing to be torn in half, the person would be squeezed tightly in the funnel of the black hole. Neil describes it like squeezing someone through a pasta machine. The process scientifically is called "spaghettification."

Black holes are hard to see because the light the dying star releases is only in the form of invisible x-rays. The Chandra X-ray Observatory is a space telescope that shows scientists where the x-ray radiation from black holes is located.

Astrophysicists were surprised to discover that all galaxies, except perhaps dwarf galaxies, have black holes at their centers. Scientists wonder if perhaps it is the extreme gravity of the black hole that pulled all the stars together to form each galaxy. The black hole in the center of a galaxy determines how the galaxy evolves as it grows by eating close stars. If it eats too many stars, the black hole is left with a small galaxy. But if a black hole gobbles up everything near it, the singularity goes out of business. With plenty of star material, a black hole can eat indefinitely.

Sometimes black holes are eating so many stars at one time that an enormous amount of light is set free as the stars are ripped apart while traveling along the event horizon before being swallowed into the singularity. These galaxies in the far distant universe shine very brightly. They are called *quasars*, and they give off more light than anything else in the cosmos. Astrophysicists have determined that these galaxies have a supermassive black hole in their centers.

Some large galaxies have more than one black hole at the center. One of the largest galaxies, Abell 2261, is thought to have two supermassive black holes at its center. Our own galaxy, the Milky Way, has one black hole at its center.

A mystery that puzzles scientists is, where does the material swallowed by the black hole go? Does all that star stuff pass through the singularity and explode out the other end into another universe? Some scientists think that other universes may have been created by other big bangs. Neil thinks this is an interesting concept, but there is no evidence for more than one universe right now. Scientists developed the "multiverse" theory to try to explain the mystery of dark energy. We cannot see other universes any more than we can look into a black hole. One way we might find out about another universe is if our universe continues to expand and bumps into something else far out in space. Scientists of the future will have to answer this question.

Fossils in Space

For now, current space scientists study the past universe to discover how it came to be. With new tools, astrophysicists try to see even farther back to the beginning of time. Paleoanthropologists are scientists who search for and study fossil bones and footprints of ancient humans to learn more about human evolution. Similarly, astrophysicists search for and study fossil gas and light from ancient galaxies to learn more about the evolution of the universe. While paleoanthropologists look back several millions of years, astrophysicists must look *billions* of years into the past.

Astrophysicists face the challenge of finding fossils of things that have not changed much in the 13.8 billion years since the big bang. With better telescopes, scientists are discovering ever older light, galaxies, and clouds of gas. The Hubble Space Telescope located the oldest known galaxy in the universe. The small, faint galaxy was formed 500 million years after the big bang, when the universe was still very young. Amazingly, its light has traveled for over 13 billion years to reach us. The photons of light from this distant galaxy are like fossils.

Other space fossils are the cosmic microwave background (CMB) and pure gas clouds in outer space containing only hydrogen and helium. The CMB was formed four hundred thousand years after the big bang, when the young universe was much hotter than it is today. It is like a fossil that gives us clues about the early history of the universe. The fossil gas clouds are from the brand-new universe right after the big bang took place and before heavier elements were constructed in stellar furnaces.

Neil reminds us that fossils found here on Earth show evidence of events in space. Layers of rock reveal changes in life before and after an asteroid impact. Large asteroids leave huge craters on our planet's surface. They also leave ancient pieces as meteorites and have been responsible for the extinction of Earth life.

If scientists find a way to see dark matter, then particles of dark matter may be like fossils, too. The big bang created dark matter at the same time as it did regular matter. Since dark matter does not interact with regular matter, it should still be the same as it was at the very beginning. With dark-matter fossils, astrophysicists might be able to learn more about the period when the brand-new universe rapidly inflated, or the moment when the big bang took place. That revelation would be as wonderful as when paleo-anthropologists definitively find fossil evidence of the first human species to walk on Earth.

Our nearest neighbor, Andromeda (M31, NGC 224), is a spiral like our Milky Way galaxy. *(Image from NASA/Hubble Telescope)*

Chapter 5

OUR HOME IN THE MILKY WAY

Ten billion years after the Milky Way formed, star formation continues today at multiple locations in our galaxy.
—Neil deGrasse Tyson and Donald Goldsmith,
Origins: Fourteen Billion Years
of Cosmic Evolution, 2004

Over 10 billion years ago, an extremely large cloud of gas began spinning in space. As the mass of gas spun faster and faster, it flattened out into a pancake-like disk. As the disk twirled in space, the gas formed into a spiraling pinwheel of stars.

That spiraling disk is our own Milky Way galaxy. Our galaxy has over 200 billion stars and spans 100,000 light-years across, but is only 1,000 light-years thick. The ancient Romans thought what they could see of our galaxy looked as if milk had been spilled across the sky. They called it *Via Lactea*, Latin for "the Milky Way."

We cannot see our entire galaxy because we live within it. We see only our small part of it. If humans were able to space travel outside our galaxy, Neil would like to journey out far enough to look down and see the entire Milky Way. Scientists have created pictures of the Milky Way based on our spiral neighbor, the Andromeda galaxy. Andromeda and the Milky Way are partners with nearby galaxies called the Local Group. There are over fifty-four galaxies in this collection. The Local Group is a subset of a larger association of at least one hundred galaxy groups known as the Virgo Supercluster.

Besides holding billions of stars, the Milky Way has gas clouds, nebulae, and satellite galaxies. About two dozen small galaxies orbit the Milky Way, in the same way moons orbit a planet. The two most important satellite galaxies are the Large Magellanic Cloud and the Small Magellanic Cloud.

The Milky Way as seen from Easter Island, with the Large and Small Magellanic Clouds on the right. *(Courtesy of Donald C. Johanson)*

Magellanic Clouds

In the early 1500s, explorer Ferdinand Magellan was searching for an ocean passage around the world. When he was below the Equator in the Southern Hemisphere, Magellan noted two white spots in the night sky and thought they were nighttime clouds. We now know these spots are not clouds but dwarf satellite galaxies. Both the Large and Small Magellanic Clouds are dwarf irregular galaxies, with no arms, each holding billions of stars. The Large Magellanic Cloud has some stars that are one hundred times bigger than our sun. The large cloud also is home to one of the most productive nurseries for infant stars, the Tarantula Nebula (30 Doradus).

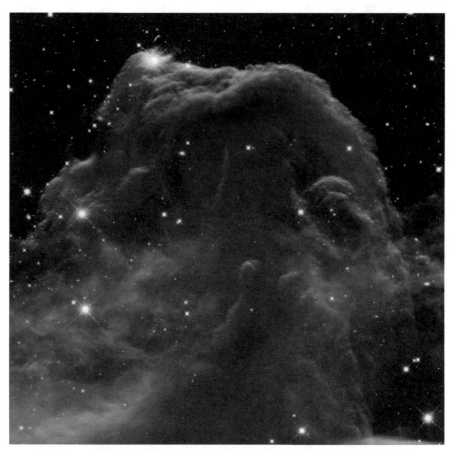

The Horsehead Nebula looks like a seahorse coming up out of the star-forming region. *(Image from NASA, ESA, and the Hubble Heritage Team [STScI, AURA])*

The Carina Nebula is full of newborn stars. *(Image from NASA, ESA, M. Livio, and the Hubble 20th Anniversary Team [STScI])*

Stellar Nurseries

Like the Tarantula Nebula, the Milky Way has several regions where new stars still are being born. In the constellation Orion, there are the Horsehead Nebula (Barnard 33) near Orion's Belt and the Orion Nebula near Orion's feet. The Orion Nebula produces thousands of stars at a time and can be seen easily through a telescope. The Carina Nebula (NGC 3372) is much larger than Orion with brighter stars, but it is not as well known because of its location in the constellation Carina in the Southern Hemisphere. The Eagle Nebula (M16) has several star-forming areas in its "Pillars of Creation." It is found in the Northern Hemisphere constellation Serpens. This "serpent" is best seen in the summer night sky.

Black Holes

Most of the Milky Way's young stars are found in the pinwheel arms of the galaxy. In the center of the galaxy is a bulge of older stars that are as old as the galaxy at 10 billion years of age. In the very center of the bulge, also at the exact center of the galaxy, is an enormous black hole. Right now, this huge black hole is inactive, as it no longer swallows nearby stars. The central black hole is called Sagittarius A* (A-Star), and it is the largest of the nineteen known black holes scattered throughout the Milky Way. Earth has nothing to fear from a black hole at present. The closest identified black hole is a small one over three thousand light-years away.

Dark Matter

The Milky Way galaxy is surrounded by a blanket of hydrogen gas. The galaxy is then wrapped with a layer of dark matter. Astrophysicists believe that this dark matter holds the galaxy together. The gravity from the stars alone would not be strong enough to keep the galaxy from flying apart as it spins.

Dark matter affects the motion of stars around the galaxy center. It influences large objects like stars and galaxies but not smaller objects such as planets and moons. Neil reassures us that dark matter does not interfere with Earth or humans as we move around on our planet's surface.

The gas pillars in the star-forming region of the Eagle Nebula (M16, NGC 6611). *(Image from NASA, ESA, STScI, J. Hester, and P. Scowen [ASU])*

Andromeda (M31, NGC 224)

The Milky Way galaxy is only one of billions of galaxies in the universe. Astrophysicists have learned a great deal about our galaxy by studying our closest neighbor, the Andromeda galaxy. This spiral galaxy is 2.4 million light-years away yet it is the farthest space object that can be seen by eye. No other galaxies are visible except with a telescope.

Everything in space is moving relative to each other. Our planet moves, the solar system moves, and galaxies move. Galaxies frequently run into each other, although the collisions last billions of years. Andromeda and the Milky Way are moving toward each other and may collide in about six billion years.[1] Astrophysicists expect that the two galaxies will pass through each other. The result will be two spiral galaxies becoming one large elliptical galaxy.

Supernovae

Astrophysicists have identified the remains of over three hundred supernovae in the Milky Way. Each one was either a huge star or

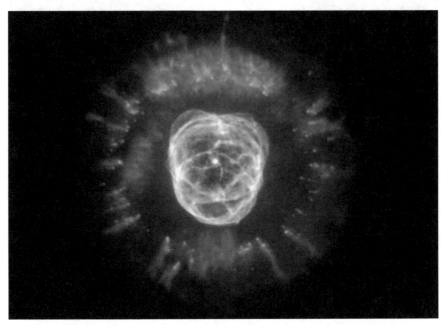

The Eskimo Nebula (NGC 2392) is a planetary nebula from a super-nova. *(Image from NASA, Andrew Fruchter, and the ERO Team)*

two smaller stars that merged and exploded, sending large amounts of gas and dust out into the galaxy. Strong winds from the explosion carry elements in the dust out into space. All these elements find their way into the molecules that make up puppies, people, and planets. As a result of supernovae, our galaxy contains a beautiful gallery of planetary nebulae, with descriptive names like the Eskimo Nebula and the Cat's Eye Nebula.

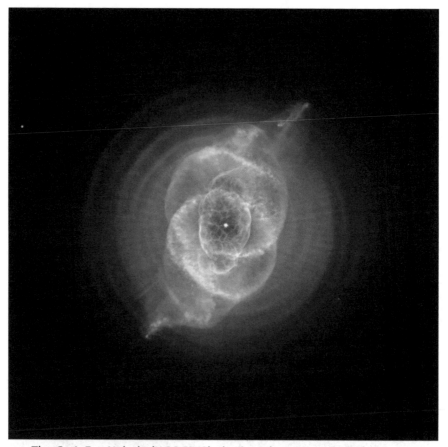

The Cat's Eye Nebula (NGC 6543) also is a planetary nebula from a supernova. *(Image from NASA, ESA, HEIC, and the Hubble Heritage Team [STScI, AURA])*

THE SOLAR SYSTEM

Five billion years ago, a star-making nebula filled with gas and dust developed in our neighborhood of space. The gas primarily was hydrogen and helium, and the dust was rich in elements such as carbon, oxygen, nitrogen, and iron that had been left by exploding supernovae. That nebula does not exist anymore, but before using up all its gas, it gave birth to our sun.

Our solar system began in similar fashion to our galaxy. A large spinning cloud of gas and dust flattened like a Frisbee. Gravity caused most of the material to gather in the center of the disk to become our sun. Typical of forming stars, enough material was left circling around the star in what is called a protoplanetary disk.

As the new sun spun, its gravity caused the protoplanetary disk to whirl around it. Within the disk, molecules of gas and particles of dust ran into each other and stuck together. Particles of dust and gas stuck together until gravity pulled them into ever-larger clumps. These clumps grew into pebbles, then rocks, and eventually planets, moons, asteroids, and comets. Most of these bodies (except for comets) orbit around the sun on the same plane and in the same direction because of their origin in the same protoplanetary disk.

The Milky Way holds us in one of its arms. Our solar system is located on the Orion spiral arm on the edge of the galaxy. We are twenty-five thousand light-years from the black hole at the center of the galaxy. The Milky Way rotates slowly in space. It takes 226 million years for our solar system to make a complete circle. That is called a galactic year. At the center of the solar system is a star, also known as the sun.

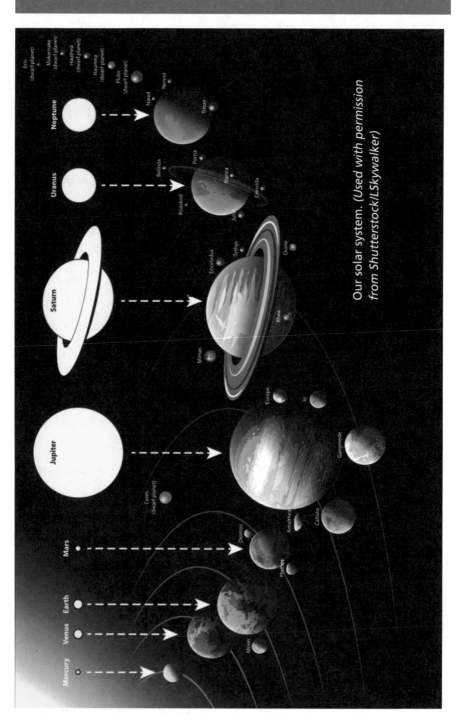

Our solar system. *(Used with permission from Shutterstock/LSkywalker)*

THE SUN

Stars can live millions, or even billions, of years. The biggest stars burn out quickly. Our sun is a middle-size average star that has been burning for five billion years. Scientists expect that our sun will burn for another five billion years. That is a very long time.

The sun is not a solid sphere. It is made of 90 percent hydrogen (H) and 10 percent helium (He). Similar to other stars, it is powered by thermonuclear fusion. Because there is so much gas in the sun, the pressure and temperature in the center are so incredibly high that atoms of H are fused together to make He.

This fusion of atoms causes a release of energy in the form of heat and light. Every time a nucleus of He is created a photon is produced. The sun is so large and the inside so violent from the fusion reaction, Neil estimates that it can take a photon of light one million years to reach the surface of the sun after forming in its center. Then, traveling at the speed of light, it takes eight minutes for that photon to shine on Earth 93 million miles (150 million kilometers) away.

Out of the Sun

The surface of the sun is quite active. Hot gases move around and sometimes shoot into space. Even back in the 1600s, Galileo noticed that there were spots on the sun. Scientists now know that sunspots are areas of cooler gases that appear darker than the rest of the surface. Once in a while gases explode on the sun and cause solar flares. Other times loops of burning gas leap up from the surface as solar prominences. These solar activities can cause power blackouts and interfere with our satellites and radio communications, causing trouble for television signals, the Internet, and airplanes here on Earth.

Charged electrical particles flow out from the sun to form the solar wind. The wind passes Earth and spreads out to the edge of the solar system. Sometimes these particles enter Earth's atmosphere near the North or South Poles and make beautiful colors in the sky. These colors are called auroras. The Northern Lights are known as Aurora Borealis, and the Southern Lights are Aurora Australis.

Some of the sun's rays are ultraviolet light that is harmful to life on Earth. We are fortunate that there is an ozone layer in the atmosphere to protect us from this light. Ozone is a molecule of three oxygen atoms. The layer of ozone in the sky helps prevent ultraviolet light from reaching the surface and damaging our skin, though some of us need sunscreen to finish the job.

Clumps

As the solar system formed, the protoplanetary disk spun quickly around the brand-new sun. Most of the hydrogen—the primary element in the universe—settled in the sun along with a good amount of helium. All the other elements from supernovae were scattered in the leftover material circling the sun. Carbon, oxygen, silicon, nitrogen, and iron bumped into each other and combined to form molecules of dust that grew into bigger clumps. Neil does not think that "clump" is a very scientific term, but it is a good description for what happened.

Eventually, the clumps arranged themselves into eight planets with moons, several dwarf planets, many asteroids, and countless comets. Essentially the solar system is divided into four small rocky inner worlds and four gas giants in the outer region. Despite being gas giants, these bodies still have a solid rocky core.

Gravity is the force that pulls objects together. The bigger an object, the greater the pull. Our sun is one hundred times heavier than all the planets combined, so its gravity can hold all the planets in orbit around the sun. The nature of each planet is determined by its distance from the sun. Closer planets orbit faster, are warmer, and have more light.

In our solar system, the sun is the only source of light. Outside the solar system, stars that make their own light twinkle for us because that light travels many billions of miles and then passes through our atmosphere. Planets do not twinkle because they are closer to us and are reflecting the sun's light back at us.

From a cloud of gas and dust (a nebula) our solar system was born over five billion years ago. Although that nebula no longer exists, the elements contained within its specks of dust were important building blocks for all things in the solar system, including ourselves. In the next two chapters, we will take a closer look at the planets and follow some of the elements from supernovae to see where they end up.

Earthrise, taken by the Apollo 8 astronauts. *(Image from NASA)*

Chapter 6

FROM DUST TO ROCKY PLANETS

Anyone will then understand with the certainty of the
senses that the Moon is by no means endowed with a
smooth and polished surface, but is rough and uneven
and, just as the face of Earth itself, crowded everywhere
with vast prominences, deep chasms, and convolutions.
—Galileo Galilei, *Sidereus Nuncius*, 1610

Mercury

Mercury is the first of the four inner rocky planets. It is the smallest planet and closest to the sun. Mercury was named for the Roman messenger god (the one with wings on his feet) because it goes around the sun quickly, orbiting once in eighty-eight days. Neil reminds us that the liquid metal, mercury, is named for the same god. Because Mercury is so close to the sun, it is eleven times hotter than Earth.

Mercury is a little bigger than our moon and resembles our moon in many ways. Meteoroids slammed into the planet's surface and left behind many wide craters like those on our moon. Also like our moon, Mercury does not have an atmosphere, so its craters are not worn down and stay the same as when they formed. Mercury does not have any moons of its own.

Mercury is so close to the sun that it is hard to see with a telescope because of the sun's brightness. Several space probes have visited the planet for a better look. NASA launched the *Messenger* (MErcury Surface, Space ENvironment, GEochemistry, and Ranging) spacecraft in 2011 to orbit Mercury. So far, astrophysicists have determined that Mercury may have a cap of water ice on its north pole. One of the specks of oxygen from a supernova likely combined with two hydrogen atoms to form a molecule of water (H_2O). The water settled on Mercury's north pole where it froze, hidden from the sun.

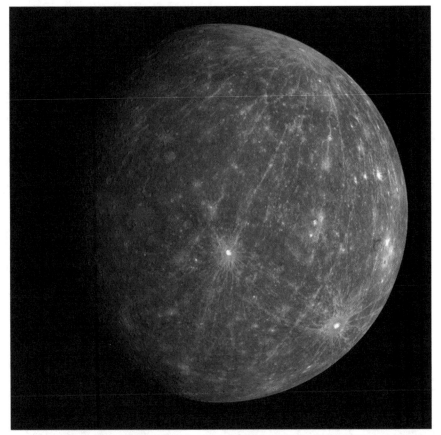

Mercury, covered with craters. *(Image from NASA, JHUAPL/Carnegie Institution of Washington)*

Venus, enveloped with thick clouds. *(Image from NSSDC Photo Gallery)*

Venus

Our closest neighbor, Venus, is Earth's sister planet. Named after the Roman goddess of love, Venus is about the same size as Earth. Like Mercury, Venus does not have a moon of its own. Even at 24 million miles away, Venus is easy to see in the sky because it is the brightest object other than the moon. Depending on the time of year, its orbit causes Venus to appear as a "morning star" or an "evening star."

Venus is so bright because the sun's light reflects intensely off the thick cloud cover of the planet. Scientists cannot see the planet's surface through the clouds. The high pressure and hot temperature of the atmosphere crushed the first space probes sent to Venus. The European Space Agency (ESA) launched the *Venus Express*, which has been orbiting the planet since 2006. It is still sending back images of the surface of Venus.

The atmosphere of Venus largely is made up of carbon dioxide. Scientists believe that Venus likely had water and oceans early in its development. The intense heat of the sun's radiation evaporated the water. Oxygen atoms from the water combined with carbon as volcanoes were erupting and filled the air with carbon dioxide (CO_2). Some of the volcanoes on Venus still might be active.

As the CO_2 built up in the atmosphere, Venus became a victim of a runaway greenhouse effect. In a greenhouse, the glass windows do not allow heat to escape. This might be good for plants, but not for a planet. The effect is called runaway because it could not stop until Venus was trapped inside thick clouds of sulfuric acid (H_2SO_4, sulfur combined with hydrogen and oxygen, which makes a corrosive acid). The clouds hold in heat like glass windows, making Venus hotter than Mercury, even though Venus is farther from the sun.

Neil considers the greenhouse effect on Venus to be a warning for Earth. As we burn more fossil fuels in the forms of oil and coal, our cars and factories add more CO_2 to our atmosphere. This increase in CO_2 causes our atmosphere to heat up and contributes to global climate change. Neil hopes Earth does not end up like Venus with no water and "hot as a furnace."

Earth

Earth is the planet about which scientists know the most. It is the most special to us because it is the only planet we know with life. The name "Earth" comes from an old English word *ertha*, meaning "ground." Earth is the largest of the inner rocky planets and is 93 million miles (150 million kilometers) from the sun. Located in what is called the "habitable zone," Earth is the proper distance from the sun for water to remain as a liquid. Scientists playfully refer to Earth as a "Goldilocks" planet: not too hot, not too cold, but just right for life to have formed 3.8 billion years ago.

Life as we know it requires liquid water to develop and survive. The water on our planet accumulated from icy comets hitting our surface and melting in the days after the formation of the solar system. Our air and water formed from the steam and gas released by ancient volcanoes.

The four elements that make up most of life on Earth are hydrogen, carbon, nitrogen, and oxygen. After helium, these are also the most abundant elements in the universe. They were born in supernovae and settled into the disk of the solar system. Along with iron, these elements are basic to our lives. Oxygen and carbon combine easily both with each other and with many other elements to fashion the foundation of living things. We breathe oxygen in the air, which mainly is composed of nitrogen. The specks of iron born from stars became both the core of our planet and a part of our blood that carries oxygen in our bodies. Of course, oxygen again combined with hydrogen to give us water.

Water exists all around in space but mainly in frozen form. Scientists assume that life starting on another planet would need liquid water. Astrophysicists are finding other Goldilocks planets orbiting distant stars. Even if we do not find other forms of life on another planet or moon in our solar system, Neil is optimistic that life may exist in the habitable zones around other stars in the universe.

As part of the wonderful diversity of life on Earth, we take an amazing journey with our planet around the sun at 66,000 miles per hour (107,000 kilometers per hour). While Earth orbits the sun, our planet also spins at 1,000 miles per hour (1,600 kilometers per hour) at the Equator, then gradually slower toward the North and South Poles. We do not feel the spin because it is so smooth and the air spins with us. Gravity holds us to Earth so we do not go flying off the surface into space.

Earth is closest to the sun in January and farthest from it in July, but this is not what causes our seasons to change. Earth's axis (an imaginary straight line connecting the North and South Poles) is at a 24-degree angle, not straight up and down. When the Northern Hemisphere of the world is tilted away from the sun, it is winter. We enjoy summer when this side of the planet is tilted toward the sun. The Southern Hemisphere experiences the opposite seasons.

Earth has one moon. Our planet maintains enough gravity to hold the moon in orbit around us. Even though the moon is one-quarter the size of Earth, its gravity is strong enough to pull on our planet. If you have been to the beach and watched the ocean tide rise and fall, then you have seen the power the moon has here on Earth.

One of Neil's favorite photographs of Earth was taken by astronauts of the Apollo 8 mission.[1] This was the first manned voyage to orbit around the moon. Called "Earthrise," the photograph shows the water, land, and clouds of our planet. It is one world undivided by boundaries between countries. Taken in the 1960s, this photograph inspired humans to start thinking about taking care of our planet and launched the environmental movement.

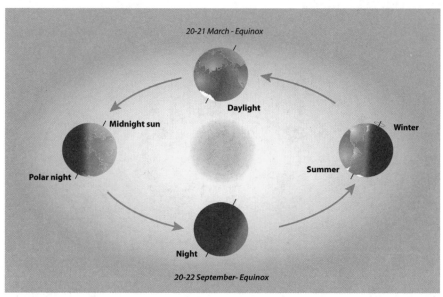

The tilt of the earth causes the change in our seasons. *(Used with permission from Shutterstock/Designua)*

Moon

We take the moon for granted because we see it in the sky all the time, just like the sun. But the moon is important to us on Earth. In addition to controlling ocean tides, the moon helps Earth keep a stable rotation. Without the moon our planet would wobble as it turned. The phases of the moon guide farmers with their planting and certain animals with their life cycles. Moonlight may provide the setting for romantic interludes, but a bright full moon interferes with telescope viewing. The moon gave us our first destination in space to dream about visiting.

Earth's moon. *(Image from NASA/JPL)*

In 1969, astronaut Neil Armstrong landed and walked on the moon as part of the Apollo 11 mission. Since 1972, people have been on the moon only five more times and no human has walked on its surface. After that, instead of people, several robotic missions were sent to the moon. Human astronauts brought back moon rocks ranging in age from 3 to 4.5 billion years old. When humans return to the moon, there will probably be more rocks that could reveal to scientists secrets about our planet in its earliest days. Scientists still study the rocks we do have to learn about how the moon formed.

MOON PHASES

Moon phases. *(Used with permission from Shutterstock/LSkywalker)*

There are several scientific opinions about how the moon came to exist. The current leading theory of the moon's formation is called the Moon Giant Impact Hypothesis. In the early days of the solar system, a great deal of debris was flying around in space. Astrophysicists believe that an object the size of Mars collided with Earth about 4.5 billion years ago. Pieces of Earth and what was left of the object flew into space and joined together by gravity to build the moon.

The name "moon" comes from the old English word for "month," which is appropriate, as the moon orbits Earth every twenty-seven days. The moon is 240,000 miles (380,000 kilometers) away, but still close enough for us to see its features by eye. The dark regions on the face of the moon are called *maria*—Latin for "seas"—because early observers thought they were bodies of water. These areas are actually dry plains. The light areas are highlands. Together, the seas and the highlands give us the iconic "Man in the Moon" face.

Many craters cover the surface of the moon. Asteroids and other large rocks traveling through interplanetary space often hit the moon, and without any wind or atmosphere to wear down the crater edges, the moon remains marked by these deep craters. Scientists suspect that some deep craters untouched by sunshine hold basins of frozen water. This ice will come in handy in the future if scientists and engineers build bases for living on the moon.

The same side of the moon always faces Earth. The moon rotates once in the same time it takes to circle the earth. The far side that we do not see is not dark because the sun does shine on it. The far side is covered in mountains and is much rougher than the side we see with its many *maria*. Neil is fond of our moon and its features because it was the first object he studied with his binoculars, just as Galileo studied the moon with his first telescope. Neil thinks the far side of the moon would be the best place for setting up telescopes. Astrophysicists would enjoy a clearer view of space than from Earth.

Our moon is not the largest moon in the solar system; there are four larger ones around Jupiter and Saturn. But it is the largest moon in relation to its planet. We have not finished exploring this brightest object in our night sky. In the future, the moon may give us valuable minerals to mine, a vacation destination, or a perfect launching base for a mission to Mars. Would you like to visit the moon and stay in a lunar hotel?

Mars

If Venus is our sister planet, then Mars is our brother. Mars is half the size of Earth. It is 142 million miles (228 million kilometers) from the sun, so it takes much longer to go around one orbit (687 Earth days). The red color of Mars inspired ancient astronomers to name Mars for the Roman god of war. Iron oxide (iron and oxygen), basically rusty dirt, coats the surface of the planet.

Mars has both smooth plains and rough meteorite-caused craters similar to those on our moon. But also it has deep valleys and high volcanoes. The Mariner Valley system of canyons is longer and deeper than Earth's Grand Canyon. Mount Olympus on Mars, now an extinct volcano, is three times as tall as our Mount Everest. That makes it the largest mountain in the solar system. Mars has two moons, Phobos and Deimos, which are probably asteroids captured by the planet's gravity.

Now cold, dusty, and barren, Mars may have supported life on it billions of years ago. Evidence suggests that water once flowed in now-dry gullies and riverbeds on the planet. What happened to all the water on Mars is a great mystery to scientists. Though water in Martian oceans evaporated a long time ago, some water may remain frozen underground as permafrost or in ice caps on the North and South Poles. Mars also had an atmosphere in ancient times, but most of that was lost. All that remains is some light carbon dioxide (CO_2).

Mars, our next destination? *(Image from NASA, ESA, the Hubble Heritage Team [STScI/AURA], J. Bell [Cornell University], and M. Wolff [Space Science Institute, Boulder])*

Why Some Space Objects Are Round

All stars are round. An object must be round to even be considered a planet. Neil describes the roundness of a sphere as the most efficient shape that an object can take. The gravity in a sphere pulls on the mass equally so that all the material wants to get as close to the center as possible. All planets and large enough moons are round. Of the known asteroids, Vesta and Ceres are the largest, and both are round. Small moons and other asteroids have weak gravity and are irregularly shaped. Spiral galaxies, such as the Milky Way, were originally spheres when they formed. As the galaxies rapidly spun, they flattened out. Neil believes that the observable universe is a sphere.

Neil considers Mars a warning to Planet Earth regarding our water supply. Some parts of Earth do not have enough fresh water for the local population. We need to appreciate how precious our water is and avoid losing it as Mars did.

While early conditions on Mars may have been favorable for life to form, scientists have not found that the cosmic elements of nitrogen, hydrogen, oxygen, and carbon came together as living organisms. That does not keep space scientists from thinking about and looking for life on Mars.

Earth has many Mars rocks, or ancient meteorites, that landed here billions of years ago. As Mars was hit by asteroids or meteor-

Rocks in Space

Asteroid: a rock or metal body, smaller than a planet but larger than a meteoroid

Meteoroid: rock or metal debris, smaller than an asteroid, usually a few feet (one meter) or less in size

Meteor: the streak of light formed by the burning meteoroid or asteroid falling through Earth's atmosphere

Meteorite: a piece of asteroid or meteoroid that survives passing through the atmosphere and lands on the ground[2]

oids, small pieces of the planet were ejected into space. Some of these rocks eventually flew our way and landed on Earth's surface. Panspermia is the idea that small particles of life from Mars were carried on these rocks and started life here on Earth. The concept of Martians visiting Earth as little green men rather than as tiny particles is a popular subject for science fiction novels and movies. Neil does not believe that any living thing could survive traveling 49 million miles (78 million kilometers) through space. Enough evidence exists for life beginning on Earth, but Neil thinks that probing out panspermia is a good reason to go to Mars and look around.[3]

Mars is the planet most frequently investigated by earthlings. So far, no humans have landed on Mars; that is a dream for the future. Instead, since the 1970s, scientists have sent many robotic vehicles to study the planet. NASA's *Mars Global Surveyor* began orbiting the planet in 1996 and has made dramatic discoveries, such as finding dry gullies that carried water long ago and taking images of frost on the South Pole. Unfortunately, its batteries ran out in 2006, so the spacecraft stopped sending information. The Mars Exploration Rover Mission delivered two rovers, *Spirit* and *Opportunity*, to Mars in 2004. These robotic vehicles traveled around the planet looking for signs of water and life. *Spirit* became stuck in the sand and ceased transmissions in 2011, but as of 2014, *Opportunity* was still driving around studying Mars.

In 2012, NASA presented an exciting mission of the Mars Science Laboratory. They showed us how the *Curiosity* rover landed safely on the Martian surface with parachutes.[4] *Curiosity* has already discovered evidence that water did indeed exist in Mars's past. Now *Curiosity* continues on its task to analyze rocks and soil for any signs of life, past or present.

Asteroids

The asteroid belt resides in a wide gap of space between Mars and Jupiter. The millions of asteroids in the belt range from tiny pea-sized rocks to large dwarf-planet size. In fact, there may be enough material to put together to form another planet, but Jupiter's huge gravity keeps the pieces from joining together into one.

Asteroids mainly are rock, but some are metal or a combination of rock and metal. Scientists tell what asteroids are made of by the way light reflects off them. Different elements in the rock or metal reflect different colors of light. Most asteroids are irregular in shape, resembling potatoes. They are too small for gravity to make them round. A few asteroids large enough to catch our attention include Ceres, Vesta, Pallas, and Hygiea. Ceres is the largest asteroid that is round and is considered a dwarf planet.

The asteroid Vesta orbits in the asteroid belt between Mars and Jupiter. *(Image from NASA/JPL-Caltech/UCLA/MPS/DLR/IDA)*

Similar to planets and moons, astronomers have named most asteroids after Greek and Roman gods and goddesses. A few asteroids are also named after artists, philosophers, and scientists. An asteroid in the main belt, discovered by David Levy and Carolyn Shoemaker, was originally called 1994KA. In November 2000, Levy and Shoemaker renamed this asteroid 13123 Tyson, in Neil's honor. Neil was relieved to learn that asteroid Tyson is not on a course to cross Earth's orbit. With thousands of asteroids, there are not enough names to go around. Most asteroids therefore are numbered and not named.

Not all asteroids are in the belt. Jupiter's gravity sometimes tugs asteroids out of the belt or nudges them toward the sun. Asteroids are also captured by the gravity of planets to become moons, such as the two of Mars or many of those around Jupiter and Saturn.

Earth occasionally is hit by stray asteroids hurtling through space. The orbits of over eight thousand asteroids pass near Earth. Most famously, an asteroid crashed into the Yucatán Peninsula in Mexico 65 million years ago. The dust from the impact likely was responsible for the extinction of the dinosaurs. Fortunately, it is more common for asteroids to fly by our planet without hitting us. In February 2013, a small asteroid blew up in the atmosphere over Chelyabinsk, Russia. It rained down many meteorites. Over one thousand people were injured by broken glass caused by the force of the explosion.

In 2005, US Congress instructed NASA to catalog near-Earth asteroids, comets, and other dangerous space objects by 2020. In 2007, NASA launched the *Dawn* mission to study asteroids in the main belt. The *Dawn* spacecraft visited Vesta in 2012 and is now on its way to Ceres.

Because they have existed since the beginning of the solar system, asteroids are like fossils. By studying the elements of asteroids, space scientists can learn about the formation of the solar system. The minerals in asteroids are of interest to private companies that would like to mine them. The importance of asteroids in the future will be more fully explored in chapter 9.

Jupiter with its moon Ganymede. *(Image from NASA, ESA, and E. Karkoschka [University of Arizona])*

Chapter 7

ICY, GAS GIANTS

Behold a majestic moonless night
Orion the Hunter rising high
Led by Jupiter in its brilliance
Across the darkened sky.
—Neil deGrasse Tyson, http://www.twitter.com,
@neiltyson, November 26, 2011

Jupiter

Appropriately, the planet that is larger than all the other planets put together is named for the king of the Roman gods. Jupiter is eleven times bigger in diameter than Earth. It also is five times farther from the sun, so it takes Jupiter twelve Earth years to circle the sun one time. Far away Jupiter is so big that it is the fourth-brightest object in our sky, after the sun, moon, and Venus, all of which are much closer.

Jupiter is a gas giant with a small core of metal and rock. The planet is made mainly of hydrogen and helium, similar to the sun. Astrophysicists call Jupiter a failed star. It just is not big enough to have the high temperatures and immense pressure needed to cause nuclear fusion to light up its gases like a star.

Jupiter emits a great deal of invisible infrared radiation. The planet sends out more energy than it receives from solar light; there are so many particles trapped in its magnetic field, and the radiation is so intense, it can damage electronic parts of space vehicles or kill people. Scientists will need to address this when astronauts are sent that far into space.

Because of its great size, Jupiter has the strongest gravity of all the planets. Comets often are pulled into Jupiter or are thrown in different directions by the strength of Jupiter's gravity. Earthlings should be grateful that Jupiter's gravity slingshots away plenty of comets and space debris heading toward us.

Jupiter is quite beautiful when viewed through a telescope. Its surface is covered with powerful storms. Probably its most famous feature, the Great Red Spot, is a hurricane twice the size of Earth that has lasted for hundreds of years.[1] The atmosphere is marked with stripes of dark, warm clouds and light, cold clouds. Jupiter has a system of thin rings surrounding the planet made up of tiny particles of sand and dust.

With sixty-five moons, Jupiter presently has more than any other planet. It trades places with Saturn concerning the most moons as new moons are discovered. There are so many moons orbiting Jupiter that space scientists think of it as a miniature solar system. We can see the four Galilean moons, named after Galileo, who discovered them, by telescope.

For seven years beginning in 1995, spacecraft *Galileo* visited Jupiter and its many moons. The mission sent back one-of-a-kind images and, with the help of several other telescopes, made amazing discoveries of a comet smashing into the planet.[2] It revealed the possibility of liquid oceans on some of the moons. Another mission by NASA, named *Juno*, is planned for 2016. *Juno* is a solar-powered spacecraft that will circle Jupiter and add to our knowledge about this magnificent orb.

The Galilean Moons

Discovered in 1610 by Galileo Galilei, the Galilean moons are the four largest of Jupiter's moons. They likely formed at the same time as the planet. The four moons are named after mythological mortals whom the god Jupiter chased after to trick into loving him. Io, Europa, and Callisto were three young maidens, while Ganymede was a young boy. Astronomers also named other moons after the god's mythical lovers.

Io (EYE-oh) is slightly bigger than Earth's moon. It is the most volcanically active world in the solar system. Hundreds of volcanoes erupt and spread sulfur over the moon's surface, giving it an orange color. Io's interior is incredibly hot because of a gravity tug-of-war between Jupiter and the other Galilean moons pulling Io in two directions.

Europa is the smallest of the four Galilean moons. Spacecraft *Galileo* discovered that Europa has a crack-lined icy crust that could be covering an ocean of liquid water. The gravitational pull of Jupiter and the other moons causes friction that keeps the water from freezing. Space scientists wonder whether there could be hot deep-sea vents similar to those supporting life in Earth's oceans. Neil would like to go ice fishing on Europa to see what sort of creature might pop up in front of his camera lens. In 2020, NASA and the European Space Agency (ESA) are planning the launch of the Europa Jupiter Space Mission to further explore Europa.

Ganymede is the largest moon in the solar system. It even is larger than Mercury and Pluto. Ganymede probably would be considered a planet if it orbited the sun instead of Jupiter. Carbon-rich rocks with a layer of water ice on top make up this moon.

Callisto is the outermost of the four moons. It is larger than Io and Europa, almost the size of Mercury. Callisto looks like our moon but with more craters. As on Europa, Callisto may have a liquid ocean beneath its surface.

Other Moons of Jupiter

New moons are constantly detected around the gas giants. Most of the other sixty-plus moons of Jupiter are smaller than the Galilean moons. The tiniest ones are probably comets and asteroids captured by the planet's gravity. The two moons closest to Jupiter are Metis and Adrastea, which are slowly orbiting closer to the planet and will eventually crash into it. Perhaps then Saturn will be able to claim first place in the race for number of moons.

Saturn, Also Known as Neil's Favorite Planet

Neil loves Saturn because of its beautiful rings—and not only because it saved him from trouble with police officers when looking through his rooftop telescope. Saturn is a gas giant similar to Jupiter. Although not as large as Jupiter, Saturn still could hold seven hundred Earths in its volume. Saturn is so far out in the solar system that it takes thirty Earth years to orbit the sun.

Named after the Roman god of agriculture, Saturn is the farthest planet we can see with our eyes. It has a small rocky core with a thick blanket of gases, mostly hydrogen and helium. Saturn does not appear as colorful as Jupiter because Saturn's cloud cover is thicker.

Saturn with an aurora glowing on its south pole. *(Image from NASA, ESA, J. Clarke [BU], and Z. Levay [STScI])*

In 1610, Galileo first saw Saturn's rings. Looking through his basic spyglass, Galileo thought the rings were two close moons that looked like ears on either side of the planet (picture Mickey Mouse). Later, with better telescopes, astronomers identified the rings.

The rings of Saturn extend out 85,000 miles (137,000 kilometers) from the planet, but they are only one mile (1.6 kilometers) thick. Astrophysicists have determined that there are seven rings separated by gaps. The rings are actually moving and are made up of particles as tiny as ice crystals and as big as icebergs. Some particles are probably broken-up moons or comets. The pull of Saturn's gravity prevents the pieces from forming together. Several tiny moons, such as Prometheus and Pandora, orbit in the rings. Gravity maintains a gap between these moons and the rings.

In his seventh-grade woodshop class, Neil designed and constructed a Saturn lamp. The light turned on and off when Saturn's wooden ring moved up and down. That special lamp sits on Neil's desk in his office and still works.

Space scientists study Saturn because its ring system is a model for the sun's ancient protoplanetary disk that formed the planets of our solar system. The *Cassini* spacecraft launched in 1997 and reached Saturn in 2004. NASA named the space mission after Giovanni Cassini, an Italian-French astronomer who discovered several moons and a large gap (also named for him) in Saturn's rings in 1695. In 2017, the *Cassini* probe is scheduled to travel between Saturn and its rings to describe the composition of the rings even better.

Saturn's Moons

The rings of Saturn are spectacular; the moons excite scientists even more. New moons are regularly discovered in the solar system because of advanced viewing technology. For a while, Saturn was ahead in the moon count, but it is now in second place to Jupiter with only sixty-two moons. Not all the moons have names. As with Jupiter, Saturn's moons are different from one another. Some moons formed with the planet, but others are asteroids or objects from the Kuiper Belt that were pulled into orbit by Saturn's strong gravity. The Kuiper Belt is the region of space outside of Neptune's orbit that is filled with hundreds of icy rocks.

Titan is the second-largest moon in the solar system, after Ganymede. It is the only moon with an atmosphere. Space scientists think that chemical processes similar to the ones that began life on Earth billions of years ago are taking place on Titan. The *Cassini* spacecraft landed the *Huygens* probe on Titan in 2005. Named after Christiaan Huygens, the Dutch astronomer who discovered Titan in 1655, the probe found organic molecules, such as carbon, that are a part of living things. Titan likely is too far from the sun and too cold for life to form. Oxygen on Titan is hidden away in water ice. Like Earth, the atmosphere is primarily nitrogen. Methane (CH_4) is a natural gas on our planet, but on Titan it is liquid. Methane rains and forms lakes on Titan's surface.

Enceladus may be Saturn's version of Jupiter's Europa because it also has liquid water under a thick surface of ice. Geysers of water shoot up from the surface of the moon like Old Faithful at Yellowstone. Enceladus is so close to Saturn that the erupting water from the moon helps to form ice in the outermost rings of the planet. With liquid water and energy provided by Saturn's gravity tugging on the moon, is it possible that some form of life could exist in warm water under the surface?

Phoebe is a tiny irregular moon that is the farthest out from Saturn. Phoebe is made more of rock than of ice when compared to the other moons. It orbits around the planet in the opposite direction from the other moons. Space scientists are eager to study Phoebe because it may be an object that escaped from the Kuiper Belt to the edge of the solar system, only to be scooped up by Saturn.

Uranus

The seventh planet from the sun is the third largest, after Jupiter and Saturn. Uranus is so far from the sun that it takes eighty-four Earth years, an older person's entire lifetime, to orbit once. The planet was named after the Greek god of the sky.

Uranus is a mysterious planet that appears blue-green through a telescope. Different from all other planets in the solar system, Uranus spins on its side. Perhaps in ancient times, a large object hit it and knocked it off-kilter. Astrophysicists see the planet's modest rings rotating up and down rather than around the middle as with Saturn. If Saturn rotates like a merry-go-round, then Uranus turns like a Ferris wheel in space.

The Hubble Space Telescope (HST) revealed a total of thirteen rings around Uranus that are thin and dark. The HST also found several new moons bringing the total to twenty-seven. Uranus's moons are named after Shakespeare characters, such as Ophelia, Juliet, Desdemona, and Prospero. The planet's atmosphere holds cosmic elements, primarily hydrogen and helium. Some of the hydrogen has combined with carbon to form clouds of methane. After discovering Uranus in 1781, scientists were puzzled by occasional changes in its orbit. That made them look for another planet farther out whose gravity must be pulling on Uranus. Scientists then found Neptune.

Uranus with its up-and-down rings and a few of its moons. *(Image from NASA and E. Karkoschka [University of Arizona])*

Neptune

Neptune was finally detected in 1846. It is even more remote than Uranus at almost three billion miles or thirty times the distance of Earth to the sun. Neptune takes 164 Earth years to orbit the sun, much longer than any human being can witness.

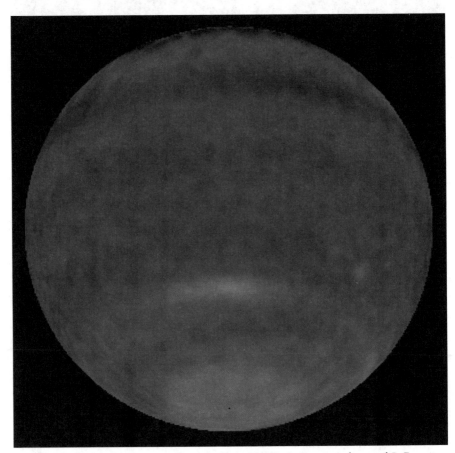

Beautiful blue Neptune. *(Image from NASA, L. Sromovsky, and P. Fry [University of Wisconsin–Madison])*

Neptune, named after the Roman god of the sea, is a beautiful blue-colored planet with wispy white clouds. The farthest planet has six faint rings made of dust. In 2013, the HST found a new moon circling Neptune, bringing the total known moons to fourteen. Triton is the largest of the moons, it is quite a bit bigger than Pluto.

Neptune's atmosphere is similar to that of Uranus—primarily methane, hydrogen, helium, and ammonia. The high amount of methane in the air reflects blue color back to us. Some scientists speculate that strong air pressure in the atmosphere might force the carbon atoms in methane to compress tightly enough together to form crystals of diamond. No one can reach Neptune yet, but if they did, the freezing poisonous air would be deadly.

Like Uranus, Neptune showed unexplained changes in its orbit. Scientists began to search for another large planet farther out. They dubbed this object "Planet X." All they were able to find was tiny Pluto.

Pluto–The Dwarf Planet

Pluto had been our ninth and farthest planet for over fifty years. It was named for the Roman god of the underworld. It has no rings but does have five moons. Charon, the largest, is almost the same size as Pluto. Four others are so tiny, they were found by the HST.

Pluto is a small, icy rock covered in frozen nitrogen, methane, and carbon monoxide (CO). It is so small that seven moons, including our own, are larger than it. Pluto is round like a planet, but it has an irregular orbit. Usually Pluto is another billion miles beyond Neptune, but occasionally it orbits inside Neptune's orbit.

In 2006, the International Astronomical Union (IAU) voted to reclassify Pluto as a dwarf planet.

The astronomer responsible for Pluto's demotion is not Neil, as many think, but Mike Brown, PhD, at the California Institute of Technology. Dr. Brown discovered Eris, an object larger than Pluto and much farther out from the sun. This discovery and the possibility of finding more objects caused the IAU to redefine what a planet is. A planet orbits around the sun, is round, and clears its orbit of other objects in its path.[3] Pluto did not meet the standards because of its irregular orbit.

Astrophysicists have found more than three hundred small, icy rocks beyond Neptune and out to the edge of the solar system. Some of them are also large enough to be dwarf planets. Beside Eris, there are Makemake (MAH-keh MAH-keh) and Haumea. Sedna is the farthest icy rock found so far, and it likely will be classified a dwarf planet. Ceres, the largest asteroid in the asteroid belt, has been designated the fifth dwarf planet.[4]

As the director of the Hayden Planetarium, Neil removed the model of Pluto from the vast planetary display in the foyer. He then received angry letters from schoolchildren complaining about Pluto's demotion from planet to dwarf planet. It was not Neil's decision, but he agreed with the IAU about reclassifying Pluto. He felt bad that schoolchildren called him a "Pluto hater." He loves Pluto as he does all parts of the universe. Neil thinks that if Pluto had feelings, it would be proud to be one of the largest objects in the Kuiper Belt instead of the puniest planet.

The Kuiper Belt

Outside the orbit of Neptune is a region of space called the Kuiper (KIGH-per) Belt. This area is a colder version of the asteroid belt. The Kuiper Belt is occupied by hundreds of icy rocks, including Pluto, Eris, and Sedna.

Orbiting five billion miles from the sun, these rocks likely are debris left over from the original protoplanetary disk that formed the solar system. Kuiper Belt Objects (KBO), as these rocks are called, never clumped together to form a planet. At present, Sedna is the farthest KBO seen by astrophysicists. Sedna marks the edge of the Kuiper Belt and the beginning of the solar system's last region, the Oort Cloud.

Dirty Snowballs in the Oort Cloud

Surrounding our solar system, the Oort Cloud may extend out into space for trillions of miles. Astrophysicists do not have as much knowledge of the Oort Cloud as they do about the Kuiper Belt. The Oort Cloud is so far into space that it is difficult to study. However, space scientists are sure that the Oort Cloud is home to billions of comets.[5]

A comet is a ball of dirt, ice, and frozen gases. Neil calls them "dirty snowballs." The ices are frozen water, ammonia, and methane, made from the basic space elements hydrogen, oxygen, nitrogen, and carbon.

Comets are small, just a few miles across in diameter. They follow a long, eccentric path around the sun. As a comet approaches the sun, the sun's heat melts some of the frozen gases. The solar wind then blows the gases and loose dust away from the comet to form its tail, which always points away from the sun whether the comet is coming or going.

Certain comets only orbit the sun once and are never seen again. These are called "new" comets. Other comets that return to the sun fairly regularly are called "periodic." Halley's Comet, probably the most famous periodic comet, flies past Earth every seventy-six years. Neil thinks new comets are more exciting than periodic comets because they usually put on a more spectacular show. New comets may take thousands of years to orbit the sun, or they may never return. After a comet circles the sun many times, its layers of ice gradually melt away. A comet is reclassified as an asteroid once it melts into rock alone.

Comet ISON in November 2013, nine days before its encounter with the sun. *(Image from NASA/MSFC/Aaron Kingery)*

Bright comets pass across our sky at least once every ten years, so you likely will see one in your lifetime. In late 2013, a comet approached Earth that space scientists hoped would be the brightest comet in centuries. A Russian astronomer discovered Comet ISON by using a telescope owned by a group of ten countries. This astronomer named the comet for the telescope, the International Scientific Optical Network (ISON). Since leaving the Oort Cloud and hurtling behind the sun, the comet returned to our neighborhood. NASA reported in December 2013 that Comet ISON broke up completely as it traveled so close around the sun, because of intense heat. Scientists still learned much about comets by watching ISON, even though the public was disappointed not to see a bright comet fly near us in the night sky.

Shooting stars or meteor showers are evidence of a comet passing through Earth's orbit. As the comet melts and releases gases, tiny pieces of dust and rock fall off the comet into its tail. These small particles burn up as they fall into Earth's atmosphere causing streaks of light that look like stars shooting across the sky. In August each year, we can see the Perseid meteor shower in the constellation Perseus. This shower marks the tail remnants of Comet Swift-Tuttle, which passes our planet every thirty years; its last visit was in 1992. The Leonid meteor shower, which takes place each November, arises in constellation Leo. Comet Tempel-Tuttle flies by every thirty years, last leaving its dust in 1998. The Geminids in constellation Gemini sparkle in the sky every December. These shooting stars are from the dust of an asteroid called Phaethon.

Comets spend most of their time in the Oort Cloud. Space scientists assume the comets that never return to the sun may have flown beyond the Oort Cloud, out of the solar system, and into outer space.

The Edge of the Solar System

There is no clear line in space where our solar system ends. The edge of the solar system is so far away that if we could travel there, our sun would just look like a bright star. All around the solar system is the heliosphere, a bubble of charged particles blown out by the solar wind from the sun. Where the sun's wind ends and the interstellar winds and star particles begin is the edge of the heliosphere.

Many years ago, NASA launched two robotic spacecraft to explore the solar system. *Pioneer 10* took off in 1972 and *Pioneer 11* in 1973. *Pioneer 10* traveled through the asteroid belt, past Jupiter, and out to the far reaches of the heliosphere. Unfortunately, its last communication was in 2003. *Pioneer 11* made it to Saturn before losing communication in 1995. Astrophysicists presume that both spacecraft now have left the solar system, but there is no way to know for sure.

In 1977, NASA launched another set of unmanned probes, *Voyager 1* and *2*, to explore the solar system. *Voyager 1* is over 11 billion miles (18 billion kilometers) from the sun. *Voyager 2* is 9 billion miles (15 billion kilometers). Scientists report that *Voyager 1*, traveling at one million miles a day, crossed from the sun's heliosphere into interstellar space in 2012. Some astrophysicists are reluctant to say that *Voyager 1* left the solar system, as it is still in the Oort Cloud. But *Voyager 1* is beyond the solar wind, so humanity can now claim to be star explorers.[6]

Launched in 2006, *New Horizons* is an unmanned spacecraft on its way to Pluto and the Kuiper Belt. NASA expects it to arrive at Pluto in 2015. *New Horizons* will then take five years to head into the Kuiper Belt to search for other icy rocks as big as or bigger than Pluto and Eris. It could take *New Horizons* another ten years to reach the Oort Cloud, so we will have to be patient and wait to learn more about what exists at the edge of our solar system.

Neil with the tools of his trade. *(Used with permission from David Gamble)*

Chapter 8

THE FATHER, THE CITIZEN, THE SCIENTIST

I am an educator and a scientist.
—Neil deGrasse Tyson, interview on C-SPAN2,
March 15, 2012

Neil is a tall, handsome African American man. He strides into his office with a friendly smile and a firm handshake. His broad shoulders are evidence of his history as an athlete. Shelves full of books and space-related knickknacks line his office walls. He displays a set of Russian nesting dolls painted with a variety of spaceships rather than the usual flowers. In addition to piles of papers, items that have special meaning cover his desk. In one corner is a container of feather quill pens. He uses these to write in calligraphy because he enjoys placing ink on paper. Sitting proudly on another corner is the lamp of Saturn he made in seventh grade. Neil presses on Saturn's rings to show how the lamp lights up.

As Neil sits down, he is obviously exhausted. He has just returned from a national tour for his most recent book. He is also filming a television series. In addition to his regular job as director of the Hayden Planetarium at the American Museum of Natural History (AMNH) in Manhattan, Neil presents speeches around the country, gives interviews for news shows, and serves on government committees. He does all this because he is committed to educating the public about space science and how the universe works. Neil wishes he had more time for scientific research, but that will have to wait until the future. Right now, any spare time he has is devoted to his family.

Family

Neil is married to Alice Young, originally from Alaska. She studied physics in Texas, however, where she and Neil met. Alice's specialty is mathematical physics. Her work is Earth-focused; she does not have her head in the stars as Neil does.

Neil and Alice have two children, a girl and a boy. Miranda and Travis are teenagers now. Neil wants them to be good students and does expect his children to go to college, but he will not mind if they choose not to be scientists. While he is not pressuring them to major in science, Neil wants his children and all American schoolchildren to become scientifically literate.

Scientifically Literate Citizens

Even a person who does not choose to be a scientist should understand basic science concepts to be an informed citizen. We all need to be aware of science issues facing us. Much political debate in our country centers around science—the use of stem cells to treat diseases, whether to address human-made climate change, and the decision to send American astronauts into space. Citizens require a solid science education to make informed decisions about current matters.

America is the most technologically advanced country the world ever has known. We should do a better job of teaching, knowing, and using science. Many people are distrustful of scientists simply because they did not learn enough basic science. Neil thinks that being literate in science protects people from false claims, such as that the burning of fossil fuels is not responsible for climate change. As carbon dioxide levels increase in our air, it is important to remember Neil's warning about Venus. Informed citizens must understand the cycle of carbon in our atmosphere and oceans. A scientifically aware public could work with governments and industries to plan a decrease in carbon dioxide levels for a future with clean air and water, with healthy animals and humans.

Some people claim that sending humans into space is a waste of money. But Neil believes that space technology and space exploration are good for a nation's spirit and economy. He even wrote a book about just that.

Writing about Space

Neil writes books and magazine articles to share his enthusiasm about the universe and to excite people about science. His most recent book is *Space Chronicles*, in which he laments the current state of America's space program. America used to be the world's leading space power in competition with the Soviet Union. Now we primarily compete with China, Japan, and India.

It has been decades since NASA has sent an astronaut into space beyond the International Space Station (ISS). Launched in 1998, the ISS circles in low Earth orbit at 230 miles (370 kilometers). On the ISS, a crew of six astronauts from a variety of countries perform important experiments. The space shuttle was used to transport our astronauts to and from the ISS. The space shuttle also carried astronauts to the Hubble Space Telescope (HST) to make repairs to it. The space shuttle program lasted from 1981 to 2011, ending without another spacecraft to take its place. We now rely upon Russian spacecraft to take our astronauts to the ISS.

No human being has walked on the moon since 1972. Neil believes that landing astronauts on the moon again will renew America's excitement for the space program. He is convinced that the far side of the moon would be a great location to set up a telescope. With barely any atmosphere on the moon, the view into space would be clear. If he could, Neil would also establish a base camp on the moon that could serve as an ideal take-off point to other destinations, such as to visit an asteroid or Mars.

At present, NASA operates several unmanned spacecraft in the solar system and one outside it. Although sending these robots is cheaper and safer than sending human beings into space, Neil wants to see a combination of both robots and people explore the solar system. For instance, he thinks humans should travel to Mars to look for evidence of life. Robots there now are performing important work, but they do not have the curiosity that people do and cannot respond to unexpected events. Furthermore, humans identify more with other humans than with machines. Perhaps people back on Earth would take more interest in manned space flights.

In his newest book, Neil appeals to America to double the rather modest budget for NASA. Space exploration would improve science education in this country as more students seek to become scientists and science teachers. All of the STEM (science, technology, engineering, and mathematics) fields will benefit. According to Neil, space technology improves the economy and our quality of life with its new inventions.

A few years after Neil became director of the Hayden Planetarium, he welcomed a new Zeiss star projector in 1999. *(Image by Denis Finnin, AMNH. Courtesy of Neil deGrasse Tyson)*

Neil has written ten books. One was an autobiography, others are informative books about the origins of the universe, black holes, and Pluto. Beginning in 1983, Neil wrote a column for *StarDate* magazine in which he answered questions about space from the general public. He did not answer as himself, though. He let his sense of humor run free as he assumed the persona of Merlin, a visiting scholar from the Andromeda galaxy. The column turned into two books, each whimsically illustrated by Neil's brother, Stephen, an artist. Neil has a large following on Twitter, but he chooses not to tweet too much complex space science information, preferring instead to share things of interest to him as they pop into his head. Recently, Neil was tickled to be included in a DC

Comics *Superman* issue. In the comic book, Neil helped Superman see his home planet around a star twenty-seven light-years away.

Talking about Space

In addition to admiring the wonders of the universe, Neil takes on the responsibility of sharing the wonders with others who do not understand how planets, stars, and galaxies work. When he was fifteen years old, Neil taught his first class to a group of adults at a nearby college. Teaching came naturally to him because "talking about the universe was like breathing." Neil now teaches at Princeton University and lectures around the world.

Neil teaches as if he is performing. With a confident baritone voice, he uses dramatic motions, gesturing with his arms and using facial expressions to show how excited he is about science. His colorful ties and vests covered with stars and planets draw audience attention. His ability to translate hard scientific concepts into understandable language, mixed with his sense of humor, keeps audiences interested.

Neil regularly appears as a science expert on national news and variety news shows. He hosted a series on Public Broadcasting Service (PBS) called *NOVA scienceNOW*. One of Neil's books, which he wrote with Donald Goldsmith, became a companion book to a four-episode show titled "Origins" on a 2004 PBS *NOVA* miniseries that he hosted. Neil currently hosts a radio talk show called *StarTalk*. He has appeared in many YouTube videos and was featured on a primetime sitcom.

Thirty-four years after Carl Sagan's *Cosmos: A Personal Voyage* informed the world about space, Neil, with Sagan's widow, Ann Druyan, was the host for the continuation of the series for a twenty-first-century audience. Released in 2014, the new *Cosmos: A Space-time Odyssey* has been updated from the original show quite a bit.[1] Neil is excited to reach out to even more people.

Space Scientist in Action

On several occasions, the US government and museums have honored Neil as an outspoken advocate of space science. As mentioned earlier, an asteroid was named after him. President George W. Bush appointed him to serve on two presidential commissions about the future of space exploration, in 2001 and in 2004. Also in 2004, NASA awarded Neil with its Distinguished Public Service Medal. This is the highest award NASA gives to a person who is not a government employee.

In 2006, NASA appointed Neil to its advisory council along with astronaut Neil Armstrong. One of the most spectacular things Neil Tyson has ever seen was the total solar eclipse when he was fourteen years old. Off the coast of western Africa in 1973, Neil boarded the *SS Canberra* to better view the eclipse. Neil Armstrong was onboard the same ship, just over three years after being the first person to set foot on the moon. Astrophysicist Neil was amazed at his good fortune to serve beside astronaut Neil. When Armstrong died in 2012, the country mourned the loss of a man who will live on in the history of space exploration.

> The great thing about being a scientist is the lens you carry with you that renders the world knowable and not so mysterious.
> —Neil deGrasse Tyson, personal interview with the author, April 25, 2012

Neil loves being an astrophysicist. He encourages his students who are considering space science to be what they want to be and not what others want for them. Neil stresses that students should learn a lot of math—the language of the universe—and realize that learning takes time.

Good scientists still are kids at heart because they never lose their curiosity and they keep asking questions. These scientists are honest and motivate themselves to learn about the universe. They do not just sit back and observe space; they invent new equipment for detecting dark matter or improve telescopes to see farther into space.

Finally, good scientists have to be able to accept criticism of their ideas and remain open-minded to new ways of thinking. For instance, when scientists reassigned Pluto as a dwarf planet, Neil saw that as a positive sign of "progress and discovery." Revisions in science result from learning more about the solar system and the universe all the time.

Neil is recognized as an expert in astrophysics outside of space science. The Museum of Science in Boston presented Neil with the Washburn Award in 2008. This award celebrates an "individual who has made an outstanding contribution toward public understanding and appreciation of science and the vital role it plays in our lives."[2]

In 2012, Neil appeared in front of the US Senate to testify about the importance of space exploration to America. His testimony is available on YouTube.

The United States Congress introduced a bill in 2013 to create the post of science laureate, someone who would be a "nationally renowned expert in their field who would travel around the country to inspire future scientists." As Neil is already fulfilling this role, the *New York Times* suggested that Congress should consider him for the post.

New York City Citizen

On the morning of September 11, 2001, Islamic terrorists crashed two hijacked airliners into the two World Trade Center towers in Manhattan. Within hours, the two buildings collapsed, killing almost three thousand innocent people and spreading debris and fear throughout New York City. Neil and his family live four blocks from the disaster area called Ground Zero. He was an eyewitness to this terrible tragedy, and dust from the collapsing buildings covered his apartment.

The Tysons safely left Manhattan to stay with Neil's parents for a while until their apartment could be thoroughly cleaned. Upon his return to Manhattan, Neil felt that he was a changed person. He hugged his children more often and was friendlier to strangers. He felt more emotional and angry, and it was easier to become sad. Neil was especially left feeling "intolerant of intolerance."

Over ten years after the events of 9/11, Neil still feels sad as he thinks frequently about the experience. Every time he hears a siren, his mind flashes back to that horrible time.

Manhattanhenge

Ancient humans constructed mysterious stone structures that were enormous. Stonehenge in southwest England is the most well known of these prehistoric monuments. Archaeologists think this structure with its ring of tall standing stones was built to mark the passing of the sun. For instance, the northeast entrance of Stonehenge matches the direction of sunrise at midsummer and sunset at midwinter. As a young scientist, Neil visited stone formations in the British Isles that are similar to Stonehenge.

Manhattanhenge. *(Courtesy of Neil deGrasse Tyson, © 2001)*

Modern humans construct tall structures of stone also. These are skyscrapers that provide offices for businesspeople and homes for city dwellers. Tall buildings that reach up to the sky are a prominent feature of New York City. The streets of Manhattan are laid out in a grid among the tall buildings. Although the skyscrapers were not built to mark the passing of the sun, Neil noticed a fascinating phenomenon with the sun in New York City. Around May 29 and again around July 12 (dates vary slightly from one year to the next), the sun sets exactly along the cross streets as if sinking into the Hudson River. Neil was reminded of Stonehenge and so named this special happening "Manhattanhenge."

Wine Connoisseur

Neil enjoys fine wine. Certain restaurants in Manhattan recognize Neil as a person with expertise in French wines. In particular, Neil's colleagues at AMNH appreciate his knowledge of wines. On occasion, Neil offers wine tastings for his grateful coworkers. Once in a while, during a wine-tasting event, Neil's friends and colleagues know him to break out his well-practiced dance moves learned in his college days.

People often associate knowledge of expensive wines with well-educated and well-cultured individuals. Years ago, when Neil was shopping, a wineshop owner treated him rudely, and he was annoyed to be regarded as someone less smart than he is. He could not help but wonder if his race played a part in that treatment.

Movie Critic

One of Neil's favorite hobbies is watching movies and finding the science mistakes. Giving moviemakers credit for a good imagination, Neil still thinks these mistakes show ignorance of science. The wrong ideas about black holes and asteroids amuse him. Many movies show spacecraft trying to fly through a wall of asteroids. In real life, spacecraft have to avoid asteroids when traveling through the asteroid belt. But the asteroids are spread out and the belt is mainly empty space.

Movies also make space sound very noisy. Outer space is actually a quiet place because it is empty of anything to carry sound waves. For drama, science fiction movies add noise where there is none.

What bothers Neil most are the dumb and unimaginative aliens that appear in film. Movie aliens usually look like humans with two arms and two eyes, and they walk on two legs. Aliens from another planet or galaxy likely would look very different from us because they evolved differently. The variety of life on Earth amazes Neil; humans look unlike many other life-forms, such as snakes and jellyfish. Alien life would have at least as much variety. Neil wishes that Hollywood could be as creative as the universe.

Notably, Neil noticed that a starry night scene in the movie *Titanic* was incorrect. He brought the error to the attention of the director, James Cameron. The movie, originally released in 1997, was rereleased in 3-D in 2012 to celebrate the fifteenth anniversary of the film and the one-hundredth anniversary of the ship's sinking. Cameron prided himself on getting everything accurate, so in the rerelease he included the correct starry sky as provided by Neil. Maybe moviemakers need to have real scientists as consultants, but then Neil would have to find another hobby.

Singing the Blues

Neil loves listening to blues music. Even though he is generally cheerful, Neil identifies with the deep feelings that life is not always sunny imparted by blues singers. The lyrics of blues songs express life's dramas of lost loves, regret, and hard living. But the singer of the blues does not stay miserable because he or she sings the blues to get rid of them.

The blues are an American music style that originated in the United States in the nineteenth century. The music of their ancestors inspired descendants of African American slaves. They sang about suffering and sadness through spirituals, ballads, and working-in-the-fields songs. By World War II, when electricity enhanced music, the blues spread out from the South and became more popular with white audiences. By the 1950s, blues music and performers were the inspiration for rhythm and blues and were the root of rock 'n' roll, which would go on to become even more popular than the blues.

Neil's favorite blues performer is Buddy Guy because he can really feel what Buddy is singing. Buddy represents the Chicago style of blues. Chicago is where many southern blacks moved to leave behind the cotton fields. Chicago blues has contributed to a mingling of the races, both on stage and in the audience. Attending a Buddy Guy concert today, one sees both black and white performers and black and white appreciative listeners.

Astrophysicist, writer, speaker, teacher, director, science expert, citizen, and father—Neil is all of these things. Is it any wonder that he gets tired sometimes? Neil does not want to slow down because "there is so much in the sky to talk about." He knows that he has fans who watch his shows, read his books, and follow him on Twitter. Neil thinks of them as "fans of space," and he is just the vehicle to convey space to the people. He fears that American science is on the decline, and he hopes through his varied efforts to "save the future."

A full-size model of the James Webb Space Telescope outside the Maryland Science Center. The telescope of the future will be launched in 2018. *(Image by the author)*

Chapter 9

DREAMS OF TOMORROW

Fully funded missions to Mars and anywhere beyond low
Earth orbit, commanded by astronauts who today would
be in middle school, would reboot America's capacity to
innovate as no other force in society can.

—Neil deGrasse Tyson,
US Senate Committee testimony, March 7, 2012

Neil wants schoolchildren to be excited about science for the future. To motivate and excite students, we need grand science projects to look forward to—projects such as going back to the moon, walking on Mars, or making sure the earth is not hit by an asteroid. Other future outstanding projects will include figuring out what dark energy and matter are, discovering more Earth-like planets, or finding evidence of life elsewhere in the universe.

Students who do not become scientists still can be excited about space science. All citizens should appreciate space and the universe in which they live. Neil believes that America has lost its "exploratory compass." He hopes that kids with their natural curiosity will lead space exploration in the future.

Why Humans Explore

Human beings explore outside their comfort zone to look for a better place to live, to claim more land, to make money, or just to discover what else is out there. Neil understands that previous space exploration in the 1960s and 1970s was driven by competition with the Soviet Union during the Cold War. Although he would like scientific curiosity to be the reason for space exploration, Neil is confident it would also be good for the American economy.

The technology invented in the earlier space race benefits us all. Global Positioning System (GPS), the satellite system we use to navigate in our cars, was first used in space. Other inventions we use frequently include pens that write upside down, cordless tools, ear thermometers, and invisible braces for our teeth.

Today Americans take for granted that humans already walked on the moon and that there are unmanned space probes visiting all the other planets in the solar system. That makes many people think we have accomplished our goals in space. But there still is so much to learn about outer space, and there are new inventions just waiting for space scientists and engineers to develop them, if we keep on exploring.

GRAND SCIENCE PROJECTS

Return to the Moon

Neil is convinced that Americans stopped dreaming about the future in space after the Apollo program ended in 1972, the last time a human being left low Earth orbit. NASA had hoped to return humans to the moon by 2020, but President Barack Obama and Congress cut the budget. A government-funded moon landing might not happen until 2030.

Not wanting to wait that long, several private companies have stepped in to develop spacecraft to carry passengers into space. People would travel either to tour or to build a base on the moon.[1]

The Apollo astronauts carried with them all the air, fuel, and water they needed while on the moon. Those resources only last a short while. Long-term travel does not allow carrying everything needed to survive. Neil says that the recent discovery of water ice in deep craters at the moon's poles will allow astronauts to carry less baggage with them in the spacecraft. Astronauts could melt and filter water ice for drinking, and they could break apart the water molecules to supply oxygen to breathe and hydrogen to use as rocket fuel.

Buzz Aldrin is a former Apollo astronaut who was the second person, after Neil Armstrong, to walk on the moon. He hopes to see fresh human footprints on the dusty surface of the moon. However, Buzz would prefer that Americans aim for Mars, so the feet do not necessarily need to belong to a US astronaut. Still, he would like to see our country leading a group of scientists, engineers, and robots from many countries working together to build a base on the moon.

An expedition to the moon is an exciting opportunity to situate a space telescope or a launching site for long-distance travel to outer space. Some dreamers envision large solar power stations on the moon. These stations could collect electricity to send to Earth and help to reduce our dependence on fossil fuels. Learning to live on the moon's surface will help astronauts prepare for more hostile environments, such as that on Mars.

Walking on Mars

> By the mid-2030s, I believe we can send humans to orbit Mars and return them safely to Earth. And a landing on Mars will follow. And I expect to be around to see it.
> —President Barack Obama,
> speech on space exploration in the
> twenty-first century, delivered April 15, 2010
>
> I have a dream that one day . . . we will walk on Mars."
> —Neil deGrasse Tyson,
> http://www.twitter.com, @neiltyson, August 26, 2013

According to Neil, it takes about nine months to travel to Mars. Though the return trip to Earth takes the same amount of time, the return has to wait until the two planets are lined up just right, making the total round-trip about three years.

Three years is a long commitment for astronauts to make to be away from home. Early Earth explorers also took years away from home to travel. Ferdinand Magellan, the Portuguese explorer for whom scientists named the Large and Small Magellanic Clouds, and his crew were the first people to circle the earth by sea. His expedition lasted for three years from 1519 to 1522.

A private group called Mars One is planning a one-way trip to Mars in 2023. They hope to build a settlement on the planet as a step into the rest of the solar system. So far, thousands of people have volunteered to be among the first inhabitants of Mars.[2] These people will have to be as brave as the Pilgrims were when they crossed the Atlantic Ocean to start a new life in a new world.

The long trip to Mars likely will result in many advances in medicine as scientists work to protect the health of space travelers. Weightlessness causes bone loss, and the high level of radiation around Mars may cause cancer. Doctors will have to invent new disease preventions and treatment solutions for these problems. Mental health professionals will look to discover breakthroughs in taking care of stress and depression associated with long times spent in the isolation of space. These future inventions and discoveries, and others not yet dreamed of, would be useful to people back home on Earth.

While the Obama administration is not interested in landing humans on the moon at present, it does support plans to head to Mars in the future. But first, President Obama would like astronauts to visit asteroids.

Asteroids

Asteroids have been in the news recently: one exploded over Russia in 2013, President Obama wants NASA scientists to capture one, and several private companies want to mine asteroids for their valuable metals. Three reasons asteroids will be important in the future are (1) to study them for science, (2) to mine them, and (3) to learn how to prevent them from crashing into Earth.

Studying Asteroids

Asteroids are little bits of rock and metal left over after the formation of the solar system 4.6 billion years ago. Studying asteroids gives space scientists a better understanding of what our solar system was like when it was brand-new.

President Obama has endorsed the idea of capturing an asteroid and pulling it into orbit around the moon.[3] Once in place, maybe by 2021, NASA astronauts would visit the asteroid and collect samples of rock for space scientists back on Earth to analyze. Scientists have not yet selected an asteroid, but they are determining which asteroids are small enough (about the length of a football field) and close enough to catch. Analyzing rock or metal samples from asteroids will help determine which asteroids would be good to mine for valuable minerals.

Mining Asteroids

Several private companies, such as SpaceX, Orbital Sciences, and Blue Origin, are partnering with NASA in developing safe spacecraft to fly to the asteroid belt.[4] Without the benefit of examining actual rock samples, space scientists were still able to figure out that valuable metals such as gold and platinum may be more abundant on asteroids than here on Earth. Of course, one of the reasons gold and platinum are valuable is because they are rare. We may see a new version of California's gold rush of the 1800s heading to the asteroid belt in the future.

Whether for the purpose of capturing or mining an asteroid, sending humans to explore asteroids would be good practice for long-distance travel and eventually going to Mars. In 2005, the Japan Aerospace Exploration Agency sent an unmanned spacecraft to an asteroid. *Hayabusa* ("Peregrine Falcon") collected some grains of dust from the surface of an asteroid and returned to Earth in 2010. In addition to finding valuable metals, space scientists hope to find water ice and other materials that would be useful for space travelers venturing that far. Scientists also may learn useful information about protecting our planet from asteroids.

Avoiding Asteroid Impacts

> Dinosaurs are extinct today because they did not build spacecraft. . . . For humans to become extinct would be the greatest tragedy in the history of life in the universe—because the reason for it would not be that we lacked the intelligence to build interplanetary spacecraft, or that we lacked an active program of space travel, but that the human species itself turned its back and chose not to fund such a survival plan.
> —Neil deGrasse Tyson, *Space Chronicles*, 2012

Meteor Crater in Arizona is almost one mile wide. It was formed by a meteor the size of a school bus fifty thousand years ago. *(Image from Smithsonian Scientific Series [1938])*

Not only does Neil like the idea of studying asteroids for science; he also wants to keep an eye on any that come into our neighborhood. Every day, over four hundred tons of space material falls to Earth. Most of the dust and pebbles burn up harmlessly in our atmosphere. Neil is concerned with the bigger rocks that could hit Earth with the force of a bomb and hurt people. Deadly asteroids only strike once in a million years. An asteroid formed Meteor Crater in Arizona fifty thousand years ago. The almost one-mile-wide impact crater illustrates the damage an asteroid can do to Earth. Neil's recent passion is setting up an early warning system for asteroids on a collision course with Earth and deflecting them before they hit us.

In February 2013, a small asteroid exploded over a city in Russia. Broken glass from the blast injured at least fifteen hundred people. The asteroid blew up in the atmosphere and left a scattering of meteorites on the ground. Shortly after that event, another asteroid zipped past Earth closer than the communication satellites that orbit our planet. These two incidents highlight why we need to identify and track the threatening asteroids and comets as they orbit too close to us in their path around the sun.

About ten thousand asteroids and comets have been designated as near-earth objects (NEO). Of these, twelve hundred are the most dangerous and are to be watched closely. Congress has ordered NASA to compile a complete catalog of NEOs by 2020. Astrophysicists expect to find many more NEOs by then.

The asteroid about which Neil is most worried is named Apophis, after the Egyptian god of darkness and destruction. In 2029, Apophis, on its way toward the sun, will zoom by Earth also closer than our satellites. When it returns in 2036, Apophis will be even closer to Earth. It is smaller than the asteroid that may have killed the dinosaurs, but it could still do terrible damage if it struck our planet.

At present, Earth scientists do not have a program to avoid asteroid impacts, but they are working on ideas. NASA and the European Space Agency (ESA) have devised three potential ways to divert incoming asteroids: (1) hit the asteroid with a heavy spacecraft to knock it off course, (2) use the gravity of a large spacecraft beside the asteroid to pull it out of orbit, or (3) blast a large asteroid with a nuclear weapon. Neil is worried that blowing up a large asteroid will cause it to break up into a bunch of little ones that will still be heading toward us. An essential part of an effective program is an early warning system in case people living in the impact area need to evacuate. An early warning system requires many more telescopes with the sole purpose of looking at asteroids. Unfortunately for the Russian citizens, no one saw that 2013 asteroid approaching.

Other space scientists join Neil in his concern about an asteroid collision. The B612 Foundation, set up by a former astronaut, is launching a space telescope in 2017 to keep a sharp eye on asteroids in our neighborhood. The foundation was named after the fictional asteroid B-612, on which the Little Prince lived. *The Little Prince* by Antoine de Saint-Exupéry is about a young alien who visits Earth and learns to appreciate his small asteroid back home. Like the Little Prince, someday human beings will walk on an asteroid, whether to study, to mine, or to deflect the asteroid.

Dark Matter

One question that Neil would like answered in his lifetime is "What is dark matter?" Astrophysicists have been searching for the answer since the 1930s and will keep looking into the future. Even though no one can see dark matter yet, space scientists can see its effects. Astrophysicists are sure that clumps of dark matter exist around galaxies because of the way the gravity of dark matter bends the light around the galaxy. Space scientists believe that dark matter holds the stars in the galaxy together. These scientists have planned new satellites and telescopes that may one day discover the first "visible" particle of dark matter.

Dark Energy

Dark energy is a mysterious force that is causing the universe to expand faster than it should. As gravity works to pull galaxies together, dark energy pushes them away from each other. Astrophysicists still do not know what dark energy is or where it comes from. They are working toward developing additional telescopes, both on land and in space, to use to better understand dark energy.

One project already under way is the Dark Energy Survey (DES). The DES is examining how the sizes and shapes of one hundred thousand galaxy clusters change over time.[5] These measurements will reveal to scientists which force is stronger in the tug-of-war between gravity and dark energy. This information will help predict the future of the universe.

Space scientists have three theories for how the universe will end. In about 100 trillion years, the fate of the universe will turn on whether gravity or dark energy is stronger. In theory 1, called the big crunch, expansion continues until dark energy runs out and gravity pulls the universe back into one tiny point. This would be the big bang in reverse. Theory 2 is the big rip, in which dark energy keeps increasing and pulls the universe apart. As this happens, the universe will become darker and colder. The Milky Way would be alone as other galaxies moved farther and farther away. The final theory is called the big chill, or "knife-edge," because it requires dark energy and gravity to balance just right. Dark energy might stay the same, with the universe slowly expanding, but it could go on forever.

Other Planets in the Galaxy

> If the sun has a planetary family, so too might other stars, with their planets equally capable of giving life to creatures of all possible forms.
> —Neil deGrasse Tyson and Donald Goldsmith,
> *Origins: Fourteen Billion Years*
> *of Cosmic Evolution*, 2004

In 1600, Giordano Bruno, an Italian friar, speculated that there are stars with orbiting planets that have life on them. Such thoughts were against the teachings of the Catholic Church, so he was burned at the stake by the Church. But humans would continue to wonder. It was not until 1995 that astronomer Geoff Marcy discovered one of the first planets orbiting a star that is not our sun. Planets that orbit other stars in our galaxy are called "exoplanets." Dr. Marcy believes there are billions of exoplanets.[6] So far space scientists such as Dr. Marcy know of almost one thousand exoplanets, although new ones are regularly discovered. Scientists are watching another two thousand possible objects to see if they also are exoplanets.

In 2009, NASA launched the Kepler Space Telescope to search the Milky Way galaxy for exoplanets the size of Earth that orbit in the habitable zone of their star. A planet the right size and the right distance from its star could have liquid water and foster life, especially if the star is like our sun. Kepler was aimed at a small area of sky and concentrated on 170,000 stars.

Exoplanets are hard to see directly because they are light-years away and do not make their own light. Astrophysicists devised two ways to find them: the transit method and the wobble method. In the transit method, as an exoplanet crosses in front of its star, the transit causes starlight to dim a tiny bit. Space scientists look for that small change in starlight to detect an exoplanet.

In the second method, the gravity of an exoplanet pulls on its star a little bit and makes it wobble. The wobble motion of the star changes its light spectrum. Recall that spectrometers break down visible light into rainbow colors. By seeing how much the color of light varies from longer wavelengths of red to shorter wavelengths of blue, astrophysicists can figure out whether a planet is orbiting that star. Using either method, Kepler's discovery of a possible exoplanet is confirmed by scientists using other space telescopes or one of the many ground-based telescopes.

At first, Kepler was only able to find very large exoplanets. These gas giants are called "hot Jupiters" because of their size and because they orbit very close to their fiery star. Scientists are certain no life could be found on them. Eventually, astrophysicists began to find smaller exoplanets, some the size of Earth. The most Earth-like exoplanet is Kepler-22b. Its star is similar to our sun, and it orbits in the star's habitable zone. However, Kepler-22b is very far away at 620 light-years' distance.

European astronomers discovered the closest Earth-size exoplanet so far. It orbits Alpha Centauri B, one of the stars in a triple-star system. The other two stars are Alpha Centauri A and Proxima Centauri, the closest star to our solar system. Alpha Centauri B is 4.3 light-years away (25 trillion miles, 41 trillion kilometers). Neil estimates it would probably take 75,000 years (equal to 1,000 generations of people) for our fastest space probe to reach Alpha Centauri. The exoplanet is closer to its star than Mercury is to our sun, so it is not in the habitable zone. Scientists will keep looking in the hope there are other exoplanets that form a solar system around Alpha Centauri B.

Debra Fischer, an astrophysicist at Yale University, first discovered a multiple-planet system around a star in 1999. Since then, several other stars in the Milky Way galaxy have been found with their own solar system. Gliese (GLEE-za) 667C is a red dwarf star not as hot as our sun but with at least six exoplanets in orbit. Three of these exoplanets are slightly larger than Earth and are in the star's habitable zone. These are excellent candidates for places with liquid water. Gliese 667C is located twenty-two light-years away in the constellation Scorpius.[7]

Elsewhere in space, the Hubble Space Telescope has found exoplanets by measuring the light reflecting off an exoplanet from its star. It revealed a beautiful, hot Jupiter-like body that is deep-blue in color. Designated HD 189733b, this exoplanet is sixty-three light-years away from Earth. It is not blue from an ocean. The exoplanet is a giant ball of gas with clouds of silicon. It is so close to its star that melted silicon falls in raindrops of liquid glass, giving the exoplanet its blue hue.

An artist's impression of the blue exoplanet HD 189733b, discovered in 2013. *(Image from NASA, ESA, M. Kornmesser)*

The Future of Exoplanets

As astrophysicists continue to find smaller exoplanets, they hope to discover exomoons as well. Space scientists already suspect that some moons in our own solar system, such as Jupiter's Europa and Saturn's Titan, could be places where life might form. Perhaps there are exomoons elsewhere capable of supporting life. Astrophysicists will need better telescopes in the future to tell for sure. More powerful telescopes will also tell more about the exoplanets already found to determine whether they are hot and dry, whether they have a solid surface or gas, or if they have an atmosphere.

Why is it important to search for exoplanets? There are two reasons. First, Earth scientists are anxious to know if life exists anywhere else in the universe. Second, scientists know the sun will burn out eventually in billions of years, and humans, or their descendants, may have to leave our solar system to live on an Earth-like planet around another star.

A star like our sun lives about 10 billion years. Scientists calculate that the sun now is five billion years old with another five billion years left to burn. In one billion years, the sun will heat up enough to boil the oceans on Earth and evaporate our atmosphere. Mars is cold now, but it would warm up then. Neil expects that earthlings will be living in colonies on Mars by that time.

After another four billion years, the sun will run out of hydrogen to burn. With only helium left, the sun will burn hotter and expand into a red giant. The red giant will be 250 times as big as the original sun and will swallow up the four inner rocky planets, including Earth. It then will be time for humans living in Martian colonies to head to the outer planets. Perhaps Europa or Titan would warm up enough to be humanity's home for a while.

Finally, the sun will become a tiny white dwarf before it goes totally dark. That will be a good time for humans to leave this solar system for an exoplanet orbiting another star similar to our sun. Neil hopes that space scientists will have found an exoplanet with the right conditions by then.

Keep in mind that five billion years is a very long time. None of us will be here to see the end of our sun. Of the over three billion years that life has existed on Earth, our species, *Homo sapiens*, has been on the planet for only two hundred thousand years. Humans still have a long future on Earth. Before worrying about the loss of our sun, earthlings should worry about real threats to our planet, such as climate change, pollution, collision with an asteroid, or destruction by nuclear weapons used in war or terrorism. These all are things about which humanity can choose to take action to prevent. Meanwhile, space scientists will keep searching for exoplanets and exomoons that may come in handy far into the future.

Unfortunately, the Kepler Telescope suffered a malfunction that cannot be fixed.[8] Before it failed, it had found thousands of exoplanets, many Earth-sized and in habitable zones, with a dozen exoplanets even smaller than Earth. NASA is unable to point the telescope, but it still can view the sky in one direction. Kepler only looks at a small section of our galaxy. Imagine how many exoplanets we might find in the rest of the Milky Way with new and better telescopes.

Some astrophysicists suspect that half the stars in the Milky Way have orbiting planets. That could mean billions of exoplanets. Of the stars that are like our sun, about one in five may harbor Earth-sized or larger exoplanets in their habitable zones. It will be up to future generations to find ways of traveling light-years to reach distant life-supporting exoplanets. With the ever-increasing number of exoplanets being found, how can life on Earth be the only life in the galaxy?

Astrobiology

> Every star may be a sun to someone.
> —Carl Sagan, *Cosmos*, 1980

The earth is not the center of the solar system. The solar system is not the center of the Milky Way. The Milky Way is not the center of the universe. Is it possible Earth still is special because it is the only place in the universe with life?

Astrobiologists are scientists looking for life on other planets or moons. They work closely with astrophysicists studying the atmospheres and surfaces of these planets and moons. Astrobiologists know that the ingredients for life exist elsewhere in the universe. They also know that they may find conditions for life elsewhere, but that does not mean that life itself exists. Conditions for life are the presence of liquid water, a form of energy like sunlight or heat, and organic molecules that contain the element carbon.

Life on Earth began 3.8 billion years ago as tiny microbes, basic one-celled organisms like bacteria. DNA (deoxyribonucleic acid) is the basis of all life on Earth. According to Neil, if we find DNA-based life on another planet, then we may be related to that life-form. If that new life-form is not DNA-based, then it began separately from life on Earth.

There are two other main ways that life elsewhere could be different from ours. Instead of carbon, life elsewhere might use another element such as silicon for the base structure of its molecules. Also, instead of liquid water, life elsewhere could be based on another liquid such as methane or ammonia. That would make for very different life, indeed!

Challenges of Extreme Conditions

Earth scientists look for life in hostile places on our planet where no one expects living things to be. Organisms that live in harsh environments on Earth are called extremophiles. Astrobiologists are interested in learning more about these creatures because there are harsh environments throughout space.

Examples of extremophiles are bacteria living near the boiling water of volcanic hydrothermal (hot water) vents on the ocean floor or in the acid water of hot sulfur springs. Scientists have discovered microbes living in deep caves without the benefit of sunlight. Even the hardest and coldest ice on Earth can support life. Algae have been found living on Antarctic ice.

The coldest place on Earth is near the South Pole beneath Antarctic ice. Scientists have detected lakes under several miles of solid ice. They are drilling through the ice to sample the water for the presence of microbes living in the cold and dark. The trick is to not contaminate the water with microbes from the surface. Astrobiologists think life could exist in the liquid water of Jupiter's moon, Europa. Learning to drill through miles of ice without introducing Earth microbes will come in handy when we send a robotic probe to Europa in the future. The northern Arctic ice of Alaska is also being studied to draw a parallel to the possibility of life on Saturn's moon, Titan.

Other extreme environments on Earth are useful to study in preparation for exploring moons and planets. If life can survive in freezing, dark, and hostile places here on Earth, perhaps it can find a way to arise in similar conditions elsewhere. For instance, microbes live in the permafrost (ground water frozen in the soil) of Siberia. This makes an excellent stand-in for examining the permafrost on Mars for life.

Intelligent Life Possibilities

Some space scientists are looking for evidence of past life on Mars, while others hope to find active life anywhere else. If found in our solar system, life likely will be tiny microbes. Out in the galaxy, astrobiologists hope that life may have evolved for billions of years as it did here. Neil is optimistic that life does exist on exoplanets in habitable zones around other stars in the universe.

If life evolved over billions of years on an exoplanet or exomoon, it could have developed into an advanced civilization like ours. In 1984, Dr. Carl Sagan cofounded the Search for Extraterrestrial Intelligence (SETI) Institute. The organization's purpose is to explore the universe for life. Known for its wide array of satellite dishes, SETI surveys the sky for radio signals that an advanced civilization on another world may have sent. SETI also sponsors projects to explore our solar system and galaxy for indications of life.

So far, space scientists have not succeeded in observing signs of life in our solar system, but they will continue to explore other planets and their promising moons. Searching for life on exoplanets and exomoons has just begun. With stronger and better telescopes, astrobiologists may find success in the future.

Future Telescopes

Since the days of Galileo and Newton, scientists have dreamed of bigger and better telescopes to see more stars and reach farther into space. As telescopes continue to be built larger and stronger, astrophysicists will learn even more about the universe.

At least three enormous ground-based telescopes are planned for the next decade. The Giant Magellan Telescope will be so powerful that scientists expect it to view exoplanets directly. This telescope will begin viewing objects from Chile in 2020. Also in Chile, scientists and engineers will build the European Extremely Large Telescope, which should be working by the early 2020s. A third telescope known as the Thirty Meter Telescope will begin operating in Mauna Kea, Hawaii, in the early 2020s as well. This telescope should take sharper pictures from the ground than the Hubble Space Telescope (HST) does now from space.

The twenty-year-old HST has provided space scientists with spectacular images of stars and galaxies. The Hubble Ultra-Deep Field (HUDF) is a photograph of a tiny area of space taken by the HST to search for the most distant, and therefore the most ancient, galaxies in the universe. The HUDF pictures ten thousand galaxies, including the oldest galaxy ever found at 13.3 billion years old. This galaxy formed when the universe was quite young, only several million years after the big bang. But space-based telescopes will be expanding as well as the land-based ones. Astrophysicists are excited about a future space telescope that will be more high-powered than the HST. The James Webb Space Telescope (JWST) is to be launched in 2018. Neil says that the "JWST's greatest value to modern astrophysics will be its ability to see so far back in time, that it can witness the formation of the galaxies themselves."[9]

The JWST is a joint effort of NASA, the European Space Agency, and the Canadian Space Agency. It is designed with a mirror that will collect the first light from far-off stars and galaxies when they formed. The large mirror is built in eighteen sections, each one covered in a thin layer of gold to collect more light. The JWST will gather visible light and invisible radiation at infrared wavelengths. This telescope will be able to identify objects through thick clouds of space dust.

Astrobiologists are also excited about the JWST. They will gather more details about known exoplanets and look for new ones.

To discover signs of life on an exoplanet, space scientists need to know what gases are in its atmosphere and which elements are on its surface. The JWST will separate the light reflected off the exoplanet from the light of its star. A built-in spectrograph will break down the exoplanet's light to determine if the molecules of life are present. With the aid of more powerful telescopes, space scientists may discover things that are not expected or even imagined yet.

Conclusion

> We're too powerful; we're too smart; we have too many ambitious people to deny our next generation the privilege of inventing tomorrow.
> —Neil deGrasse Tyson, *Space Chronicles*, 2012

We use science and technology every day. It is important to understand basic science concepts, whether one is a future scientist or a concerned citizen. Either way, we are lucky to be living at a time when science makes new discoveries in space every day.

Thanks to astrophysicists like Neil, we know more about those twinkling points of light than our ancient ancestors ever could conceive. Neil thinks that science has only begun to figure out the universe. He says, "We don't have all the answers for now so we must be content with the questions themselves."[10] There still is much left to learn about outer space. This book is just a beginning, a brief introduction to the universe to inspire further research. We need to support more scientists who specialize in studying space, people who want to work with sophisticated equipment. But we also need greater involvement of regular people who enjoy astronomy as a hobby, amateurs working with a good pair of binoculars or a telescope.

Many people only look at the night sky through apps on their smartphones or tablets, if they look at all. Neil wants students to turn off their TVs and electronic devices and go outside to wonder at the stars and the planets. While it takes many years to become an astrophysicist, one does not require a college degree to explore space with a telescope. Amateurs often spot objects such as asteroids and comets while scientists are busy looking at other things in the galaxy.

Today's students are the next generation of astronauts, engineers, space scientists, and space tourists. Some dreamers foresee hotels on the moon and cruise ships among the planets. These things can happen only if we dream big about the future. Space belongs to everyone. It is so big that it can handle the big new ideas the next generation will dream of for tomorrow.

We share DNA with every living thing about which we know. That makes us genetically connected to all creatures on Earth. Now we know we also are chemically connected to all objects in the universe. Realizing that each of us carries the universe within us gives Neil a comforting sense of belonging to something bigger than himself.

To all students—stay curious, keep dreaming, and as Neil says often, "Keep looking up!"

ACKNOWLEDGMENTS

This book would not have happened without the help of Neil deGrasse Tyson. I give a special thank you to Neil for meeting with me and answering my many questions. Our meeting took place because of the helpful assistance of my dear friend Dr. Ian Tattersall at the American Museum of Natural History. Neil's executive assistant, Elizabeth Stachow, facilitated communicating with and procuring photographs from Neil.

Thank you to Dr. Henry Ferguson at the Space Telescope Science Institute (STScI) for reviewing the scientific information. Dr. Frank Summers, also at STScI, inspired me with his monthly space lectures at Johns Hopkins University and gave me advice about how to obtain the best-quality images from the Hubble Space Telescope gallery. The staff of the Kitt Peak Observatory in Arizona contributed to my research, and I thank them for showing me the four Galilean moons of Jupiter, my favorite planet.

My husband, Pete, accompanied me to the top of Kitt Peak, but I am most grateful for his editing of my manuscript. Pete, and our daughter, Megan Molitoris, read every word from start to finish. My favorite fifth-grade teacher, Jamie Nicholson, read the final version of the manuscript to make sure it was on a middle-school reading level. My good friend Frank Kollman helped me improve the quality of several photographs. Another dear friend,

Dr. Donald Johanson, generously shared an excellent photograph of the Milky Way with the Large and Small Magellanic Clouds. Don is the subject of my first book *The Lucy Man: The Scientist Who Found the Most Famous Fossil Ever!*

I appreciate the suggestions regarding this book that were offered by these children's writers—Mary Bowman-Kruhm, Minnie Gallman, Sue Poduska, and Debra Shumaker—members of our nonfiction critique group under the aegis of the Society of Children's Book Writers and Illustrators.

NOTES

CHAPTER 1: A YOUNG SCIENTIST LOOKS AT THE SKY

1. To find out more about the Explorers Club, visit the organization's website at http://www.explorers.org.

2. To hear this in Neil's own words, watch http://www.youtube.com/watch?v=CtWB90bVUO8.

3. To learn more about how Neil became a noted scientist, read his autobiography, *The Sky Is Not the Limit* (Amherst, NY: Prometheus Books, 2004).

4. To discover more about the Hayden Planetarium at the American Museum of Natural History in New York City, go to its website at http://www.haydenplanetarium.org.

CHAPTER 2: A SPACE SCIENTIST GROWS UP

1. The history of the National Aeronautics and Space Administration (NASA) is available through its website, http://history.nasa.gov.

2. NASA's first African American astronaut was Guion (Guy) Bluford Jr., born in 1942. America's first woman in space was Sally Ride (1951–2012). Read her new biography *Sally Ride*, by Lynn Sherr (New York: Simon & Schuster, 2014). Russia had two noteworthy women cosmonauts: in 1963, Valentina Tereshkova was the first woman in space; and in 1984, Svetlana Savitskaya was the first woman to walk in space.

3. *Cosmos: A Personal Voyage*, the 1980 PBS television series by Carl Sagan, still is available as a book or on video.

CHAPTER 3: LOOKING AT ALL BEAUTIFUL THINGS

1. Hubble's discovery was a surprise because, at first, Einstein changed his theory of general relativity to show that the universe was not moving. After seeing Hubble's work, Einstein revised his theory to agree with the expansion of the universe. Claire Datnow, *Edwin*

Hubble: Discoverer of Galaxies (Springfield, NJ: Enslow, 2001), p. 84.

2. Read about other remarkable women astronomers in Mabel Armstrong, *Women Astronomers: Reaching for the Stars* (Oregon: Stone Pine, 2008).

3. As quoted in Stephen Hawking, ed., *On the Shoulders of Giants* (Philadelphia: Running Press, 2002), p. ix.

4. Neil deGrasse Tyson, *Universe Down to Earth* (New York: Columbia University Press, 1994), p. 28.

CHAPTER 4: THE EVOLUTION OF NEIL'S FAVORITE UNIVERSE

1. For a free sky map to see the constellations, go to http://www.kidsastronomy.com.

2. A list of Messier's objects is available through Astronomy Source, http://www.astronomysource.com/messier-catalog/.

3. For more detail on the expanding universe, visit http://www.nasa.gov/astrophysics/focus-areas/what-is-dark-energy.

CHAPTER 5: OUR HOME IN THE MILKY WAY

1. To watch a short video animation of the Milky Way and Andromeda colliding in about six billion years, go to HubbleSite's "Cosmic Collisions Galore!" April 24, 2008, News Release Number STScI-2008-16, "http://hubblesite.org/newscenter/archive/releases/2008/16/video/a/ (accessed November 12, 2014).

CHAPTER 6: FROM DUST TO ROCKY PLANETS

1. Apollo 8 was the first of NASA's manned probes to orbit the moon in 1968. Apollo 11 was the first manned moon landing in 1969. To read more about these missions, visit NASA's website detailing the Apollo program, http://www.nasa.gov/mission_pages/apollo/missions.

2. If you think you saw a meteor or found a meteorite, visit the American Meteor Society at http://www.amsmeteors.org.

3. Panspermia is described in more detail in Neil deGrasse Tyson, *The Sky Is Not the*

Limit (Amherst, NY: Prometheus Books, 2004), p. 170.

4. The video of *Curiosity* landing on Mars can be seen on NASA/Jet Propulsion Laboratory's website at "Curiosity Has Landed," August 6, 2012, http://www.jpl.nasa.gov/video/index.php?id=1103 (accessed November 12, 2014).

CHAPTER 7: ICY, GAS GIANTS

1. The Hubble Space Telescope recently reported that the Great Red Spot is now smaller. Scientists will try to determine if the storm is weakening. HubbleSite, "Hubble Shows That Jupiter's Great Red Spot Is Smaller Than Ever Seen Before," May 15, 2014, News Release Number STScI-2014-24, http://www.hubblesite.org/newscenter/archive/releases/2014/24 (accessed November 12, 2014).

2. Pictures of Comet Shoemaker-Levy 9 smashing into Jupiter are available at "Video IP1 12 Comet Shoemaker-Levy Collides with Jupiter," YouTube video, 1:19, posted by "SH1R33N," December 11, 2008, http://www.youtube.com/watch?v=CiLNxZbpP20 (accessed November 24, 2014).

3. How to define a planet is explained at "Pluto and the Developing Landscape of Our Solar System," International Astronomical Union, at http://www.iau.org/public/themes/pluto/.

4. As of 2008, the IAU recognizes five named dwarf planets.

5. More information on the Oort Cloud is found in Neil deGrasse Tyson and Donald Goldsmith, *Origins: Fourteen Billion Years of Cosmic Evolution* (New York: W. W. Norton & Co., 2004).

6. You can follow the two *Voyagers* through space at NASA/Jet Propulsion Laboratory's "Voyager: The Interstellar Mission," website, http://voyager.jpl.nasa.gov.

CHAPTER 8: THE FATHER, THE CITIZEN, THE SCIENTIST

1. *Cosmos: A Spacetime Odyssey*, hosted by Neil, aired in thirteen episodes on Fox and National Geographic networks, from March 2014 to June 2014.

2. Information about the Washburn Award presented to Neil by the Museum of Science in Boston can be found at Museum of Science, "Washburn Award," http://www.mos.org/washburn-award.

CHAPTER 9: DREAMS OF TOMORROW

1. Former astronaut Buzz Aldrin advocates for building a base on the moon in his book *Mission to Mars* (Washington, DC: National Geographic, 2013).

2. Read about Mars One's mission to send humans to Mars at http://www.mars-one .com.

3. To see NASA's plans to capture an asteroid, watch the NASA video "Animation of Proposed Asteroid Retrieval Mission" hosted by Space.com at http://www.space. com/20601-animation-of-proposed-asteroid-retrieval-mission-video.html   (accessed November 12, 2014).

4. NASA discusses its partnerships with private companies at "NASA Commercial Crew Partners Continue System Advancements," http://www.nasa.gov/content/nasa -commercial-crew-partners-continue-system-advancements/.

5. Follow the work of scientists conducting the Dark Energy Survey (DES) at http:// www.darkenergysurvey.org.

6. To learn more about how Dr. Geoff Marcy discovers exoplanets, read Vicki Oransky Wittenstein, *Planet Hunter* (Honesdale, PA: Boyds Mills Press, 2010).

7. Compare some of the more common exoplanet systems, including Gliese 667C, in Rick Johnson and Roen Kelly, "Exoplanet Systems Illustrated," *Astronomy* 42, no. 12 (December 2014): 44–45.

8. Even though the Kepler Telescope is not working as it was designed, it continues to help space scientists discover new objects. Kepler-10c is a rocky exoplanet that is being called a "Mega-Earth" because it is seventeen times the mass of our planet. Kepler-10c orbits a star 560 light-years away. Harvard-Smithsonian Center for Astrophysics, "Astronomers Find a New Type of Planet: The 'Mega-Earth,'" June 2, 2014, Release Number 2014-14, http:// www.cfa.harvard.edu/news/2014-14 (accessed November 12, 2014).

9. Neil deGrasse Tyson, personal e-mail exchange with the author, October 4, 2013.

10. Neil deGrasse Tyson, *My Favorite Universe* (Chantilly, VA: Teaching Company, 2003), lecture 7.

GLOSSARY

asteroid. A chunk of rock and/or metal left over from the formation of the solar system; most asteroids are between Mars and Jupiter in the asteroid belt.

astrobiology. The study of whether life exists in the universe outside of Earth.

astronomical unit (AU). Distance from the sun to the earth, 93 million miles (150 million kilometers), used to measure distances in our solar system.

astronomy. The study of the past, present, and future of space and everything in it.

astrophysicist. A scientist who studies all the objects in the universe, including planets, moons, comets, asteroids, stars, and the space in between.

big bang. The theory that all energy and matter in the universe began in an explosion followed by rapid expansion 13.8 billion years ago; this expansion continues today.

black hole. Product of the collapse of a very large star whose gravity is so intense nothing nearby can escape, including light.

Cepheid. A pulsating star that flickers regularly, used to measure distances between galaxies.

comet. A "dirty snowball" made of dirt, ice, and frozen gases that orbits the sun from as far out as the Oort Cloud; a tail forms as it nears the sun and the ice melts. The solar wind then blows the gases and dust away.

constellation. A group of stars as seen from the earth that resembles the pattern of an object, animal or mythological character after which it is named; the night sky is divided into eighty-eight constellations.

cosmic microwave background (CMB). Radiation expressed in microwaves and radio waves that represents light left over from the big bang.

cosmologist. A scientist who studies the structure and evolution of the universe.

cosmos. The universe and its processes as a whole.

dark energy. A mysterious antigravity force that causes the universe to expand at a faster and faster rate.

dark matter. Physical particles that do not give off light and cannot yet be seen by scientific instruments but that exert gravity on space objects, the effect of which can be observed.

dwarf planet. A space object orbiting the sun that resembles a planet because it is round, but is too small to have enough gravity to clear other objects from its orbit.

electromagnetic spectrum. The whole range of photons from the low frequency of radio waves up to the highest frequency of gamma waves; includes visible light.

element. Basic constituents of all matter; there are ninety-eight natural elements in the universe, the smallest is hydrogen (H), the largest is uranium (U). Additional elements are human-made in a laboratory.

exoplanet. Planet that orbits a star outside our solar system.

extremophiles. Organisms that live in harsh environments on Earth, giving hope to space scientists that life could exist on other worlds.

galaxy. A large group of millions or billions of stars, along with additional gas and dust, held by gravity and traveling together through space.

gravity. The force of attraction between objects based on their mass and the distance between them.

habitable zone. The area around a star in which a planet or moon can orbit and maintain liquid water, making it capable of supporting life as we know it.

heliosphere. The region of space around the sun that contains our solar system, and through which the solar wind blows.

interstellar. The space between the stars.

Kuiper Belt. The area of our solar system beyond Neptune containing objects made of rock and ice left over from the formation of the solar system, Pluto is one of the largest objects.

light. Made up of particles of energy called photons, light is radiation of differing wavelengths along the electromagnetic spectrum.

light pollution. Human-made light that interferes with people or telescopes viewing space objects through Earth's atmosphere.

light-year. The distance light travels in one year, six trillion miles (10 trillion kilometers), used to measure great distances in space.

meteor. A streak of light passing through Earth's atmosphere as a space object such as a meteoroid burns up.

meteorite. A piece of asteroid or space rock that does not burn up through the atmosphere and lands on Earth.

meteoroid. Rock or metal space debris that is smaller than an asteroid.

moon. A natural satellite that orbits a larger object such as a planet, dwarf planet, or asteroid.

multiverse. An unproved theory that our universe is just one of many.

nebula. A cloud of gas and dust in space lit up by new stars being formed inside; a stellar nursery.

Oort Cloud. The region on the edge of our solar system beyond Pluto that holds billions of comets.

ozone. A molecule in Earth's atmosphere that protects us from harmful ultraviolet radiation. Three oxygen atoms combine to make one molecule of ozone (O_3).

panspermia. The theory that the source life on Earth may have been carried here by asteroids or comets.

photon. Basic particle of light, it has no mass but acts as both a particle and a wave of energy.

planet. An object orbiting a star that meets three criteria: is large enough to be round, does not have thermonuclear fusion, and has enough gravity to clear its orbit of other objects.

planetary nebula. The gas shell left behind after a large star explodes and dies, creating a beautiful image that has nothing to do with planets.

protoplanetary disk. The flat area of gas and dust formed around a new star from which planets and other objects form.

red shift. Description of wavelengths of light become longer as a radiating object gets farther away.

space dust. Atoms of elements that combine into molecules as gases in stars cool; the heavier elements clump together into larger particles to become the building blocks for space objects.

space-time. Mathematical combination of space and time, used to describe events with both the dimensions of space and time together.

spectrograph. An instrument that separates a light wave into a spectrum; for instance, visible light is separated into the rainbow spectrum.

spectrometer. An instrument that measures properties of light, such as intensity.

star. A mass of gas held together by gravity large enough to have thermonuclear fusion take place at its center, causing it to release energy as light and heat.

supernova. Explosion of a massive star so strong that elements heavier than iron are fused and sent out into space.

telescope. An instrument to observe objects in space by collecting different wavelengths of light using lenses and/or mirrors.

thermonuclear fusion. In the presence of high temperatures, the combining of the nuclei of smaller atoms to form larger atoms resulting in the release of energy.

universe. Everything that exists in space-time, including all matter and energy.

visible light. The type of light that exists in the electromagnetic spectrum that human eyes can see, light that can be broken down into the colors of the rainbow.

BIBLIOGRAPHY

BOOKS

Aldrin, Buzz. *Mission to Mars*. Washington, DC: National Geographic, 2013.

Armstrong, Mabel. *Women Astronomers: Reaching for the Stars*. OR: Stone Pine Press, 2008.

Aronson, Marc. *If Stones Could Speak: Unlocking the Secrets of Stonehenge*. Washington, DC: National Geographic, 2010.

Asirvatham, Sandy. *The History of the Blues*. Philadelphia: Chelsea House, 2003.

Bernstein, Carl. *A Woman in Charge*. New York: Alfred A. Knopf, 2007.

Branch, Taylor. *At Canaan's Edge: America in the King Years*. New York: Simon & Schuster, 2006.

Brown, Mike. *How I Killed Pluto and Why It Had It Coming*. New York: Spiegel & Grau Trade Paperbacks, 2012.

Datnow, Claire. *Edwin Hubble: Discoverer of Galaxies*. Springfield, NJ: Enslow, 2001.

Davidson, Keay. *Carl Sagan: A Life*. New York: John Wiley & Sons, 1999.

Dickinson, Terence. *The Universe and Beyond*. 5th ed. Buffalo, NY: Firefly Books, 2010.

Ellis, Carol. *Wrestling*. New York: Marshall Cavendish, 2011.

Galilei, Galileo. *Sidereus Nuncius*. Translated by Albert Van Helden. Chicago: University of Chicago, 1989.

Hawking, Stephen, ed. *On the Shoulders of Giants*. Philadelphia: Running Press, 2002.

Hoskin, Michael. *Discoverers of the Universe: William and Caroline Herschel*. Princeton, NJ: Princeton University Press, 2011.

Mandel, Howard, ed. *The Billboard Illustrated Encyclopedia of Jazz and Blues.* New York: Watson-Guptill, 2005.

Maran, S. P., and L. A. Marschall. *Galileo's New Universe.* Dallas: BenBella, 2009.

Newton, Isaac. *Principia.* Edited by Stephen Hawking. Philadelphia: Running Press, 2002.

Northrop Grumman. *Space Primer.* Northrop Grumman Space Technology, 2009.

Sagan, Carl. *Cosmos.* New York: Random House, 1980.

Saint-Exupéry, Antoine de. *The Little Prince.* New York: Harcourt, Brace & World, 1943.

Sobel, Dava. *A More Perfect Heaven.* New York: Walker & Co., 2011.

Steele, Philip. *Isaac Newton: The Scientist Who Changed Everything.* Washington, DC: National Geographic, 2007.

Stowell, L., and P. Allen. *The Story of Astronomy and Space.* London: Usborne, 2009.

Trefil, James. *Space Atlas.* Washington, DC: National Geographic, 2012.

Tyson, Neil deGrasse. *Death by Black Hole.* New York: W. W. Norton, 2007.

———. *Just Visiting This Planet.* New York: Doubleday, 1998.

———. *Merlin's Tour of the Universe.* New York: Doubleday, 1997.

———. *The Sky Is Not the Limit.* Amherst, NY: Prometheus Books, 2004.

———. *Space Chronicles.* New York: W. W. Norton, 2012.

———. *Universe Down to Earth.* New York: Columbia University Press, 1994.

Tyson, Neil deGrasse, C. Liu, and R. Irion. *One Universe: At Home in the Cosmos.* Washington, DC: Joseph Henry Press, 2000.

Tyson, Neil deGrasse, and Donald Goldsmith. *Origins: Fourteen Billion Years of Cosmic Evolution.* New York: W. W. Norton, 2004.

Wittenstein, Vicki Oransky. *Planet Hunter.* Honesdale, PA: Boyds Mills Press, 2010.

Yeomans, Donald K. *Comets: A Chronological History of Observation, Science, Myth, and Folklore.* New York: John Wiley & Sons, 1991.

ARTICLES

Bakich, Michael E. "Voyager's 'New' Solar System." *Astronomy* 41, no. 1 (January 2003): 30–35.

Carroll, Sean. "Digging Up the Early Universe." *Discover* (July/August 2012): 72–74.

Cowen, Ron. "Galaxy Hunters." *National Geographic* (February 2003): 2–29.

Croswell, Ken. "Heart of the Milky Way." *National Geographic* 218, no. 6 (December 2010): 92–99.

Finkbeiner, Ann. "Galaxy Formation: The New Milky Way." *Nature* 490 (October 2012): 24–27.

Johnson, Rick, and Roen Kelly. "Exoplanet Systems Illustrated." *Astronomy* 42, no. 12 (December 2014): 44–45.

MEDIA

The Leonard Lopate Show. WNYC, Public Radio. April 28, 2002.

Tyson, Neil deGrasse. *My Favorite Universe.* Chantilly, VA: Teaching Company, 2003. Film.

YouTube. A variety of interviews with and lectures by Neil deGrasse Tyson are available at http://www.youtube.com.

WEBSITES

American Meteor Society, www.amsmeteors.org

"Ask an Astrophysicist," http://imagine.gsfc.nasa.gov/docs/ask_astro/ask_an_astronomer.html

Astronomy magazine's Site for Kids, www.astronomy.com/kids

Chandra X-ray Observatory, http://chandra.harvard.edu/index_kids.html

Dark Energy Survey, www.darkenergysurvey.org

European Space Agency, www.esa.int/

Hayden Planetarium, www.amnh.org/our-research/hayden-planetarium

Hubble Space Telescope, either http://hubblesite.org or www.nasa.gov/hubble

International Astronomical Union, http://iau.org

Mars Exploration, either www.mars-one.com/ or www.exploremars.org

NASA Earth Observatory, http://earthobservatory.nasa.gov

NASA/Jet Propulsion Laboratory, http://www.jpl.nasa.gov/

NASA Science Astrophysics, http://www.nasa.gov/astrophysics/focus-areas/what-is-dark-energy

NASA for Students, http://www.nasa.gov/audience/forstudents

Planetary Society, www.planetary.org

Search for Extraterrestrial Intelligence, www.seti.org

Sloan Digital Sky Survey, www.sdss.org

Space News, www.space.com

Virtual Astronomical Observatory, www.virtualobservatory.org

Zooniverse for citizen scientists, www.zooniverse.org

INDEX

Page numbers in **boldface** refer to photographs and illustrations.

ABOUT THE AUTHOR

CAP Saucier is a freelance writer and illustrator of non-fiction material for children. She is a former pediatric nurse who has always loved science. CAP has traveled around the world exploring the wonders of Europe, Central and South America, and several countries in Africa. She counts many scientists among her friends.

Neil deGrasse Tyson with the author.
Photo by the author.

In her first book, *The Lucy Man: The Scientist Who Found the Most Famous Fossil Ever!*, CAP wrote about Dr. Donald Johanson, the noted paleoanthropologist who discovered our ancient human ancestor *Australopithecus afarensis*, known as Lucy. When Dr. Johanson received the Explorers Club Medal in 2010, CAP was fortunate to be introduced to Dr. Neil deGrasse Tyson at the ceremony. The idea to write about Neil began at this meeting.

CAP serves on the board of the Institute of Human Origins at Arizona State University. Read about her adventures on her website, http://www.capsaucier.com.